MW01452900

Hope for Tomorrow, Peace for Today

A collection of poems and devotionals, reflections and meditations

Carol J. Grace

author**HOUSE**

AuthorHouse™
1663 Liberty Drive
Bloomington, IN 47403
www.authorhouse.com
Phone: 833-262-8899

© 2024 Carol J. Grace. All rights reserved.

No part of this book may be reproduced, stored in a retrieval system, or transmitted by any means without the written permission of the author.

Published by AuthorHouse 10/01/2024

ISBN: 979-8-8230-3194-3 (sc)
ISBN: 979-8-8230-3195-0 (e)

Library of Congress Control Number: 2024917979

Print information available on the last page.

Any people depicted in stock imagery provided by Getty Images are models, and such images are being used for illustrative purposes only. Certain stock imagery © Getty Images.

This book is printed on acid-free paper.

Because of the dynamic nature of the Internet, any web addresses or links contained in this book may have changed since publication and may no longer be valid. The views expressed in this work are solely those of the author and do not necessarily reflect the views of the publisher, and the publisher hereby disclaims any responsibility for them.

Contents

Comments from Readers xi
Foreword xiii
Preface xv
Introduction xvii

Prayer 1
Original Sin 2
It is all about Grace 4
The Voice of Our Lord God 5
Like the Sound of Many Waters 6
Move That Fence, Neighbor 8
Another Barrier 9
The Potter and the Clay 11
A Holy People, A Chosen People 13
Come 15
Move that Bushel! 16
He Knelt Down for Me 20
Grace, Mercy and Pardon 22
Shattering the Darkness 25
Catching the Vision 26
Finish Your Work in Me 29
Touching the Hem of His Garment 30
The Parable of the Just 33
The Justice of God 35
Time to Plant 37
A New Day 38
No More a Little White Lie 40
A Life of Balance 41

The Lord is Countin' on You	44
Come to the Table	45
Through a Child's Eyes	49
Who is Jesus to You	50
Straight to the Heart	53
Sing with Gratitude	54
The Journey Always Takes You Home	56
The Parable of the Prodigal	57
Reflections of a Life Well Spent	61
Jonah, Jeremiah, and Habakkuk	62
Redeemed	65
A Tale of Two Men	66
Seeing what Abraham saw	69
The Majesty of God	70
The Star-thrower	72
Knowing Jesus	73
I was there	75
The Resurrection of Jesus	77
The Nature of Faith	81
A Faith More Precious than Gold	82
Developing Hind's Feet	85
The Call to Follow	87
Rise up	89
Intentional Discipleship	91
Who is this God?	93
The Importance of Hymns	95
We're Only Human	97
Blessed is He who comes in the Name of the Lord	99
A Journey of Faith	102
Letting Go	103

    Turning Point 106
    Longing For God 108
    Rapture Ready 110
    And the Angels Rejoiced 111
    Going Home (For Pa) 116
    Life in the Spirit.. 117
    A Mother's Heart 121
    A Steadfast Love 123
WHAT IS PRAYER? 125
    The Gap 127
    Standing in the Gap... 128
    They Just Sang Praises... 130
    Singing in the Storm 131
And Then There is Hope 134
    Hope.. 136
    The Red Thread 137
    Bring them in, Build them up, Send them out 140
    Come and see...Go and Tell 142
    Build Yourself Up 147
    For Such a Time as This 150
    Get Ready! 152
    Blessed Are They 154
    Changing our Attitude.. 155
    Living by Faith 158
    Hope In the Lord 159
    Hope, pray, believe.. 161
Grace offers hope, and hope leads to peace..................... 163
    The Big Picture 166
    Yet I Will Rejoice 167
    The Gospel of Peace... 169

Perfect Peace 170
Seeking Peace 172
What Would Happen? 174
Humble Yourself 175
On Higher Ground 176
Be Strong 177
Two hundred feet ahead 178
The Brokenness of Sin 180
Never Give Up 182
Choosing God 183
Perspective 185
Be Kind 186

Poetry in Memoriam 187
You're Going to Miss Me When I'm Gone 188
His Little Corner of the World 189
Gathering Eggs 190
Lake Nixon 191
The Blue Room 192
I'll Fly Away 193
My, how she loved to dance 194
Going to sleep and waking up in Heaven 196
Don't Cry for Me 197
A Glimpse into Heaven 198
Where Sickness and Death are no More 200
Val 201
For Patti 202
Sundown 203
Alyssa's Light 204
The Cowboy Code 205
The Tie that Binds 206
A Quiet Strength 207

Final Words 208
  Joy Unspeakable 208
  Faith Added to Works 209
  Driving Directions 212
  Jehovah Nissi, our Banner 213

The Final Goodbye 215

Comments from Readers

In *Hope for Tomorrow, Peace for Today*, Rev. Carol Grace offers readers a delightful walk with God through her poetry and devotionals. Each one is filled with depth, insight, and inspiration. Her book is a blessing of peace and hope to be cherished and shared.

    Rhona Weaver, *A Noble Calling*,
Award winning author and Christy Award Finalist (Evangelical Christian Publisher Association)

I have known Carol Grace for approximately 10 years and have come to see her as the upbeat, kind, and godly woman that she is. Her devotion and joy are infectious and serves her well in her mission to strengthen and edify others- just as Christ intended her to do.

Carol's second book of poetry, *More than a Memory*, put on display her spiritual depth and talent, along with the evidence of her close relationship with God. In reading samples from her newest offering, *Hope for Tomorrow, Peace for Today*, it becomes apparent that her poetry, devotions, reflections, and meditations found within this book will benefit many on their spiritual journey - beginning with me…

    Dale L Richardson
Ordained Elder/Pastor
The Global Methodist Church

Foreword

I met Carol Grace for the first time in 2023, and what an inspirational addition she has been to our church family and to me personally. She is as genuine and kind as any Christian woman I've ever known. But she is more than that. Carol is a true theologian of the best kind, with the ability to articulate the theology of God as a Divine tapestry, addressing life's deepest questions from the brokenness of life.

In the Bible we read where persons' names were changed to better describe their essence or nature. Thus, I'd suggest Carol's middle name be changed to "Of;" for she is a Carol OF Grace, a song OF God's faithful love, a melody OF His tender mercy. It is who she is.

In *Hope for Tomorrow, Peace for Today* Carol writes as a modern Psalmist with poetry and meditations drawn from her own intimate encounters with Holy God. Her poem, *The Voice of our Lord God*, and accompanying meditation, *Like the Sound of Many Waters*, remind us that true hope and peace is not superficial, but only found in the depth of the holiness of Almighty God. Listen for His voice as you read this book, and the words on these pages will resonate with your soul.

Greg Kirksey, Teaching Pastor and Chancellor, Immerse Institute, Church at Rock Creek

Preface

The Word instructs us to draw near to God. To accomplish this, I begin my morning by opening either my Bible or a Bible app, reading a passage, praying, and then writing a devotional.

I am an intentional disciple, and as such I am purposeful in learning about, aligning with, and abiding in God's presence. Seeking holiness is not a passive effort, nor is it something one can do without thinking.

As I think of God's holiness and pray that I would likewise be holy, I find that my choices are changing. No longer can I respond with anger if someone tries to bait me into an argument. Instead of staying at home on days when I do not feel well, I find myself attending church and feeling better for it.

I cannot make myself holy, or perfect, or godly. God alone does the work. This book will attempt to explore through Scripture, devotionals, and poetry the part of our Christian walk that deals with becoming sanctified, or set apart, for God.

We will never achieve human perfection, but as we strive to attain holiness, we will be perfected in Christian love. Join me, won't you, for a journey into a deeper discipleship whereby we follow God's command, "I am holy, be thou holy likewise." For it is only through walking daily with our Lord that we will find *Hope for Tomorrow, Peace for Today.*

Introduction

In this, my third book, I departed from my usual genre of poetry and included scripture and devotionals in my collection. Some of these pieces I wrote thirty years ago, and others as recently as this year.

I love poetry. I love the way there is a cadence with each line, and each stanza, filling the space in the room and in my heart. There is a power behind the words and an empowerment in probing everyday occurrences to find the beauty within.

Poetry is the ability to tell a story with an economy of words. The lines may rhyme, but not necessarily. There will be a distinct meter, and the words will paint a picture as vivid as any painting committed to canvas.

I have been writing poetry all of my life, and I started writing devotionals when we lived in Richmond, VA in the nineties. Hope for Tomorrow is a collection of poems, devotionals, and scripture.

Writing these pieces has helped strengthen my faith, and I pray that as you read this book, perhaps with Bible in hand, you will be touched by the content, and encouraged to find hope and peace which you can then share with others.

Prayer

Almighty God, you are the one true and the Living God,
Because you are a covenant making and a
Covenant keeping God, I will always
Delight in your presence.
Each day I seek you out early and you are
Faithful to answer when I call out your name.
Grant me the ability to
Hear the sound of your voice.
I want nothing more than to
Join others in corporate praise.
Keep me ever mindful of your
Laws and precepts, and
May I ever be thankful that
No law is greater than your grace.
Open my eyes and my ears to
Perceive your will,
Quench the thirst I have for you,
Receive me into your presence.
Still my fears, and
Turn my face ever toward you.
Use me as you see fit as your
Vessel, and help me to
Wait upon you.
eXamine my heart and restore to me the passion of my
Youth that I might accomplish your will with
Zeal and unwavering dedication.
In Jesus' name, Amen.

(Known as an ABC prayer.)

Original Sin

By nature, we are wholly corrupted,
by grace we are holy renewed.
Salvation came down to sinners,
and we now have a new attitude.

Writings abound of human nature,
how fair and loving we can be.
But if we fall victim to that lethal lie
we are no better than the beasts, don't you see?

God sees man through eyes that are holy
and finds no good within him,
he is evil continually from his youth,
without Jesus man's prospects are dim.

God cannot compromise on holiness.
He requires it of you and of me.
Because of our nature we cannot become
the people God wants us to be.

So, God in His love sent a Savior,
to pardon and reconcile man,
setting the captives free from sin
was part of the Master Plan.

Though we will always have a sin nature
by grace we can overcome
and yield to the call of the Savior,
living eternally in the light of the Son.

(A found poem uses other source material to create a new, original poem. Based on John Wesley's sermon "Original Sin.")

It is all about Grace

Grace, the unmerited favor God bestows on each of us so that we can respond to His call for salvation, is present while we are yet in the womb. God initiates everything needed for redemption, including paying the price for our salvation with His only Son, and because of this grace we are able to respond.

It is this prevenient grace that covers babies until they reach an age where they can respond to God's call. John Wesley called it "preventing grace."

Once we reach the age where we can answer Jesus' invitation to "Come," justifying grace redeems us from our sins and reconciles us to our Heavenly Father. As a child I learned that "justified" meant "just as if I'd" never sinned. How can that be? Because, when we ask for forgiveness, our sins are covered by the blood of Jesus.

Finally, it is sanctifying grace that gives intentional disciples the ability to walk a life of holiness. It enables us to walk through the lowest valleys and climb the highest pinnacles.

It really is all about grace

The Voice of Our Lord God

Like the sound of many
waters, is the
voice
of our Lord God.

Not the playful sound of the babbling brook,
nor the sound of rain as it hits the roof,
not the sound of the bathwater circling the drain,
nor the sound of the steam as it powers the train.

His is the voice that penetrates my soul,
His is the voice that makes me whole.
His is the voice that cures every ill,
His is the voice, that I hear still.

Like the sound of many waters, is the
voice
of our Lord God.

Like the Sound of Many Waters

Revelation 19:6 (NRSV) 6 Then I heard what seemed to be the voice of a great multitude, like the sound of many waters and like the sound of mighty thunder peals, crying out, "Hallelujah! For the Lord our God the Almighty reigns".

John 10:1 (NRSV) 1 "Very truly, I tell you, anyone who does not enter the sheepfold by the gate but climbs in by another way is a thief and a bandit. 2 The one who enters by the gate is the shepherd of the sheep. 3 The gatekeeper opens the gate for him, and the sheep hear his voice. He calls his own sheep by name and leads them out. 4 When he has brought out all his own, he goes ahead of them, and the sheep follow him because they know his voice.

Today we hear the sound of many voices, so many that it is difficult to distinguish between them all. Yet, Jesus said we would always know the sound of His voice, and we have found this to be true.

I have always loved the symbolism in John 10. The sheepfold was built for one express purpose, to keep the sheep safe. The shepherd would gather the sheep into the enclosure, and then he would lie down in the entrance so that nothing could enter or exit without his knowledge.

Sometimes, more than one flock would be kept in the same enclosure. But there would be no difficulty in bringing the sheep out because the sheep recognized the sound of the shepherd's voice and would follow only him.

And unlike cattle who are driven to their destination from behind, the shepherd leads his flock. Jesus warned of religious leaders who achieved status by deception or manipulation. The Pharisees were prime examples of those who knew the law, but they did not understand grace. They were like overlords who drove people to obedience, instead of shepherds who led them in love.

As I reflect on this scripture, I realize it is not just the sound, or the tenor, of someone's voice that makes it so familiar, it is the content of what is said. Jesus will always speak truth, but truth will be spoken in love. If we are hearing condemnation, we are not hearing the voice of Jesus. If we are hearing words that cause doubt or fear, we are not hearing the voice of Jesus.

Listen for the voice that is like the sound of many waters. It will be a refreshing sound; it will be a sound that will drown out the negativity so that joy can come bubbling to the surface of your very being. That still, small, voice of which Elijah spoke will become like a thundering waterfall of grace and mercy when we focus on God instead of the world and its problems.

Chorus
Let the water flow, flow within me
Precious holy spirit, set my spirit free
Place within my heart, a brand new melody.
Holy spirit breathe on me.

In the name of the Father, and of the Son, and of the Holy Spirit. Amen

Move That Fence, Neighbor

When Robert Frost proclaimed,
"a fence good neighbors make,"
he was purportedly quoting a
neighbor,
one who preferred walls
to wide, open pastures.

But one questions, in building
walls, are we keeping others out
or ourselves in?
Do we
even know? And then, I ask,
does anyone even care?

Another Barrier

Eph 2:4 (ESV) But God, being rich in mercy, because of the great love with which he loved us, 5 even when we were dead in our trespasses, made us alive together with Christ—by grace you have been saved— 6 and raised us up with him and seated us with him in the heavenly places in Christ Jesus, 7 so that in the coming ages he might show the immeasurable riches of his grace in kindness toward us in Christ Jesus.

In William Barclay's study of the book of Ephesians, he tells this story:

In France some soldiers along with their sergeant brought the body of a dead comrade to a French cemetery to have him buried. The priest told them gently that he was bound to ask if their comrade had been a baptized adherent of the Roman Catholic church. They said they did not know. The priest said he was very sorry, but in that case, he could not permit burial in his churchyard. So, the soldiers took their comrade and sadly buried him just outside the fence.

The next day they came back to ensure that the grave was all right and to their astonishment, could not find it. Search as they might they could locate no trace of the freshly dug soil. As they were about to leave in bewilderment the priest came up. He told them that his heart had been troubled because of his refusal to allow their dead comrade to be buried in the churchyard; so, early in the morning, he had risen from his bed and with his own hands had moved the fence to include the body of the soldier who had died for France.

That's what love can do. Rules and regulations put up the fence, but love moved it.

When we start moving fences with our own hands, then we will know we are becoming holy. When we cannot rest because of a wrong done to our fellow man, when we must rise from our beds in the early morning hours to right that wrong, we will then know the holiness of God.

In the name of the Father, and of the Son, and of the Holy Spirit. Amen.

The Potter and the Clay

The clay on the wheel was marred,
seemingly beyond repair
but the Potter molded, shaped, and perfected
until a treasure was displayed there.

The clay on the table was misshapen,
and there was nothing left to do,
but break it apart and start over again,
for the clay was too brittle to use.

But the Potter had a secret,
and only a few were aware
that clay dried out by the elements
could be revived to something beyond compare.

He dipped his hands in water,
and a transformation took place,
for a masterpiece turned its visage
toward heaven, no longer a thing abased.

We are that same ruined clay,
seeking a form of cheap grace,
but the Potter dips his hands in the water of the Spirit,
and we are reformed, no longer a disgrace.

For kingdom people need kingdom understanding,
and we need to turn each day,
to the call of the Holy Spirit as He washes
our imperfections away.

We must recognize there is a covenant,
a holy promise we are called to obey,
if we are to be molded and shaped
by His love, and more than a lump of clay.

A Holy People, A Chosen People

1 Peter 1:13 (NASB) Therefore, prepare your minds for action; be self-controlled; set your hope fully on the grace to be given you when Jesus Christ is revealed. 14 As obedient children do not conform to the evil desires you had when you lived in ignorance. 15 But just as he who called you is holy, so be holy in all you do; 16 for it is written: "Be holy, because I am holy."

Holiness is a characteristic of God. He says repeatedly, "I am holy, be thou holy, too." What is holiness? Holiness is not following laws and rules–that is legalism. Holiness is not thinking you are better than others–that is being judgmental. Holiness is that sacredness that sets us apart for God.

Why does holiness matter? Because people are all, by nature, "dead in sin," and, consequently, "children of wrath." We are justified by faith alone. And faith produces inward and outward holiness.

Inward and outward holiness. What does that mean to you? For me, it is simple: We can not just talk the talk, we must walk the walk. We might almost replace holiness with wholeness, completeness. We sense the holiness of God, and we respond to His call upon our life. Holiness should not be a burden we bear with sadness, but a mantle we wear with gladness, for to be holy is to be more Christlike in everything we do.

There should be a definitive difference between the lives of Christians and the lives of the unchurched and unsaved. May we, each day, resolve to live in alignment with God's will and His purpose.

In the name of the Father, and of the Son, and of the Holy Spirit. Amen.

Come

Jesus preaching, disciples teaching,
light revealed, truth not concealed.
But called to heed salvation's plan,
called to save the souls of man.
So now the battle rages on,
now the victory is almost won.
Come redeemer take Your place.
Come to save the human race.

Move that Bushel!

Matthew 5:14-16 (KJV) 14 Ye are the light of the world. A city that is set on a hill cannot be hid. 15 Neither do men light a candle, and put it under a bushel, but on a candlestick; and it giveth light unto all that are in the house. 16 Let your light so shine before men, that they may see your good works, and glorify your Father which is in heaven.

Was anyone here afraid of the dark as a child? I was. We didn't have a light switch in the kitchen. We had to reach across the kitchen table to a string that was attached to a light bulb in the ceiling. It was hard for me, being vertically challenged, and I remember groping for the string, and sometimes when I did reach it, in desperation, I pulled too hard, and the string broke, leaving me in darkness.

In today's scripture, Jesus is delivering His Sermon on the Mount and He talks about the light and the darkness. To whom is He speaking? To ordinary, everyday people. He didn't call just a few people aside while the rest were eating fish and bread. He was speaking to every man, woman and child on that mountain.

You see, the world was in spiritual darkness, but Jesus, the true light, was telling the folks in the crowd that day that they had a purpose, and it was to shine a light into the darkness—not just any old light. It was the light of Jesus Christ himself.

Jesus said more than once, "you have heard it said, but I say..." Whenever He said this, He was correcting a Mosaic law that had been misinterpreted by the religious leaders of the day. The Sermon on the Mount, like everything else Jesus said and did, was life changing in its content. Before, it had been taught that people were rich because God was happy with them. Conversely, they were cursed with poverty if they angered God,

Jesus changed the dynamic completely. Jesus said blessed are the poor, not in earthly possessions but in spirit. When we can recognize how spiritually bankrupt we are apart from God, then we will mourn and then, God can give us the riches of salvation.

One of the names of Jesus is light of the world. What is so special about light? Light is the great revealer. Don't want to see the dust on the furniture? Turn the lights down. Looking for the back of your earring? Turn the lights up. Only want to be a Sunday Christian? Keep the dimmer switch on. God forbid!

Jesus said when you have a light, you don't keep it to yourself by hiding it under a basket. Not only is it selfish to hide the light from others, it's useless. You might be able to see a few streams of light coming out, but a little light can actually be dangerous. A little light can cast shadows which can trip you up and make you fall. And a little spiritual light can do the very same thing.

The light in my kitchen only got rid of the darkness when it was burning. The light within us is only good when we allow Christ to shine through us.

When people see us, they should see Christ within us. They should see something different in our talk, our walk, everything about us should reflect Christ. How does that happen? Because when we begin to spend more time with Christ, then more of His light shines upon us and our light gets just a little bit brighter and a little bit stronger. And before long, everything we do reflects the light of Christ.

The world has always gotten it wrong. We emerged from the Dark Ages into the Age of Enlightenment, and from that day forward people have believed that knowledge will solve all of the world's problems. But some people have never understood that our head knowledge will never be enough. We must have heart knowledge, the knowledge of who God is and who we are in Him. The light of Jesus Christ can not be extinguished.

And what is the final reason to let your light shine? The last verse of our scripture tells us. 16 Let your light so shine before men, that they may see your good works, and glorify your Father which is in Heaven.

When people see the light within us, whether it is a smile, a kind word, or a helping hand, then we are not just helping our fellow man, we are glorifying God. And what happens when we glorify God? Not only are we transformed but all of those around us can be transformed by that marvelous light.

Isaiah 60

Arise, shine, for your light has come,
    and the glory of the Lord has risen upon you.
2 For behold, darkness shall cover the earth,
    and thick darkness the peoples;
but the Lord will arise upon you,
    and his glory will be seen upon you.

So, move that bushel, ya'll, and let your light shine!

In the name of the Father, and of the Son, and of the Holy Spirit. Amen.

He Knelt Down for Me

The woman, caught in her sin,
knew she was going to die,
yet Jesus wrote on the ground
a still unknown reply.

He knelt down for me.

The crowd demanded stoning,
after all it was the law,
but Jesus continued writing
for He quickly saw the flaw.

He knelt down for me.

The people read the words
Jesus wrote for all to see.
Were they words of forgiveness?
Did they include you and me?

He knelt down for me.

Or did He remind them
what the law really said,
that both guilty parties
would be stoned until dead?

He knelt down for me.

Then He issued one last challenge
to he who has no sin,
pick up the stone and cast it,
the crowd then quickly thinned.

He knelt down for me.

To the woman he said with kindness,
"Go and sin no more."
To me the message is still the same
and His grace still freely pours

to cover my sin and sorrow
and to enable me to forgive,
to leave the stone not cast, not thrown,
so that sinners redeemed could live.

Grace, Mercy and Pardon

Titus 3:3 (NIV) At one time we too were foolish, disobedient, deceived and enslaved by all kinds of passions and pleasures. We lived in malice and envy, being hated and hating one another. 4 But when the kindness and love of God our Savior appeared, 5 he saved us, not because of righteous things we had done, but because of his mercy. He saved us through the washing of rebirth and renewal by the Holy Spirit, 6 whom he poured out on us generously through Jesus Christ our Savior, 7 so that, having been justified by his grace, we might become heirs having the hope of eternal life.

"Years I spent in vanity and pride
Caring not my Lord was crucified
Knowing not it was for me He died
At Calvary.
Mercy there was great and grace was free
Pardon there was multiplied to me
There my burdened soul found liberty
At Calvary."

I don't know if William Newell got any of his inspiration for his song, "At Calvary", from this verse in Titus, but it certainly fits. Titus is one of Paul's pastoral letters. The pastoral letters of 1 & 2 Timothy, Philemon and Titus are called that because, unlike the epistles, these letters are not written for the body of believers but instead, to these specific leaders. But, although these letters are more personal in nature, as with all of the Bible, we can find inspiration and instruction.

Paul reminds Titus of their background. You see, Paul knew that sometimes Christ followers need to be reminded that God didn't call us because we were righteous, He made us righteous after He called us.

How much of this letter can apply to us today? All of it. If we are still foolish, disobedient, deceived and enslaved by all kinds of passions and pleasures, if we still live in malice and envy, hating one another, stirring up strife, then have we really received salvation? If we are manipulative, selfish, or if we choose lies over the truth, then what good is our salvation?

We must be willing to kneel at the cross as many times as it is needed. Why? Because it is in the shadow of the cross where our sins are covered, it is in the shadow of the cross where we learn humility, and it is in the shadow of the cross where we receive our freedom.

"Now I've giv'n to Jesus everything,
Now I gladly own Him as my King,
Now my raptured soul can only sing
Of Calvary!"

After William Newell found Christ, he sat down and wrote the words to "At Calvary." A music teacher at Moody, Daniel Towner, wrote the music, and the song was created.

There comes a time when we must put aside the things of our childhood. Holding grudges, childish. Lying when the truth would serve us better, childish. Coming to church only if we have nothing better to do, childish.

We are heirs to the promise of eternal life. Let us purpose to act like it.

In the name of the Father, and of the Son, and of the Holy Spirit. Amen.

Shattering the Darkness

Darkness, only a pinpoint,
hardly discernible,
then, darkness does
what darkness does.

Spreading, black as cancer,
morphing into the monster
it really is, snuffing out
the light and hope with it.

Prayer, only a thought
barely formed,
then, whispered in the
night, searching for light.

Faith, only a seed seeking
fertile, life sustaining soil,
growing into a mighty
weapon that pierces

the darkness, and light
streams in, filtered at
first and then prayer
joins faith and hope

is restored, darkness
overcome, shattered
by the trinity of faith,
hope and prayer.

Catching the Vision

Isaiah 6 (NRSV) 1 In the year that King Uzziah died, I saw the Lord sitting on a throne, high and lofty; and the hem of his robe filled the temple. 2 Seraphs were in attendance above him; each had six wings: with two they covered their faces, and with two they covered their feet, and with two they flew. 3 And one called to another and said:
"Holy, holy, holy is the LORD of hosts;
the whole earth is full of his glory."
4 The pivots on the thresholds shook at the voices of those who called, and the house filled with smoke. 5 And I said: "Woe is me! I am lost, for I am a man of unclean lips, and I live among a people of unclean lips; yet my eyes have seen the King, the LORD of hosts!"
6 Then one of the seraphs flew to me, holding a live coal that had been taken from the altar with a pair of tongs. 7 The seraph touched my mouth with it and said: "Now that this has touched your lips, your guilt has departed and your sin is blotted out." 8 Then I heard the voice of the Lord saying, "Whom shall I send, and who will go for us?" And I said, "Here am I; send me!"

I have always been drawn to Isaiah's description of God. He is not just holy, but holy times three! He does not occupy a small place in a small room, but His presence fills the Temple. And Isaiah, when confronted by a holy God, comes face to face with his sin. He has the only response imaginable—he accepts salvation and follows God.

But as I read Isaiah's description of the holiness of God, I wonder how many understand the importance of holiness. And I wonder how we, in the 21st century, can catch the vision of holiness.

Holiness is not discussed much in today's world, nor is it a much sought after quality. What is holiness? Simply put, holiness is being set apart. Jesus' example taught us that while we live in this world, we are not to become a part of this world. The last prayer Jesus prayed over His disciples was this: John 17 (NRSV) 15 I am not asking you to take them out of the world, but I ask you to protect them from the evil one. 16 They do not belong to the world, just as I do not belong to the world.

Yet, the lines between holiness and worldliness seem to have blurred. How do we recapture the vision? Allow me to remind you that sin entered the world through disobedience. What caused Eve to give in to the temptation of sin? Eve lingered in the vicinity of the tree with the forbidden fruit. She could have chosen to bypass the tree, but the more that she saw the fruit was good, the stronger her urge was to consume the fruit.

What if we made the decision to seek after holiness by lingering in the presence of God? What if we, the Church, committed to being intentional in following and living like the Christ? What if we neither gave in to the allure of sin, nor rejoiced in pronouncing judgment over those who do so, but instead we sought after a holy God with all of our heart, soul, mind and strength?

There is a vision that each one of us can catch. It is a vision of the most high God exemplifying holiness and inviting us to come along, to linger in His presence, to be set apart.

Psalm 27(NRSV) 4 One thing I asked of the LORD,
that will I seek after:
to live in the house of the LORD
all the days of my life,
to behold the beauty of the LORD,
and to inquire in his temple.

In the name of the Father, and of the Son and of the Holy Spirit. Amen

Finish Your Work in Me

If I can just touch the hem of his garment
I will be healed.
If He will just speak words of comfort
With His peace I will be filled.
For this the day, this is the hour
That my faith will set me free—
Jesus, finish Your work in me.

Touching the Hem of His Garment

(NIV) Luke 8:40 Now when Jesus returned, a crowd welcomed him, for they were all expecting him. 41 Then a man named Jairus, a synagogue leader, came and fell at Jesus' feet, pleading with him to come to his house 42 because his only daughter, a girl of about twelve, was dying. As Jesus was on his way, the crowds almost crushed him. 43 And a woman was there who had been subject to bleeding for twelve years, but no one could heal her. 44 She came up behind him and touched the edge of his cloak, and immediately her bleeding stopped.
45 "Who touched me?" Jesus asked.
When they all denied it, Peter said, "Master, the people are crowding and pressing against you."
46 But Jesus said, "Someone touched me; I know that power has gone out from me."
47 Then the woman, seeing that she could not go unnoticed, came trembling and fell at his feet. In the presence of all the people, she told why she had touched him and how she had been instantly healed. 48 Then he said to her, "Daughter, your faith has healed you. Go in peace."

Think of the time when you first understood that Jesus was Your Savior. For some this understanding came gradually, and for others it happened suddenly. At some point you came to the front of the church and proclaimed your faith, and shortly afterwards you were baptized. You were probably excited and just a little bit frightened, but you understood deep within you the importance of making your faith known. So it was with the woman in our scripture today.

We find in Matthew, Mark and Luke, a woman who suffered from an illness for 12 years heard that Jesus was coming. She had gone to doctor after doctor, spent all of her money and was still not healed. Somehow, she worked her way through the crowds and still she could not touch Jesus. She reached out and touched just the tassels of his garment.

Now, there was fringe at the bottom portion of the shawl and attached to this fringe were tassels representing the 613 laws found in the Torah. When the woman touched Jesus' garment, He felt some of His healing power leave Him. So He turned, and said who touched me.

I can hear someone saying, are you nuts? There is no way to know who touched you in this mob. But the woman admitted it was her. Why? She could easily have disappeared into the crowd. But she had been healed. She had to proclaim it.
There are some lessons you and I can learn from this woman.

Don't let unanswered prayers take away your hope.
Sometimes the answer is not "no," but "not now."
Regardless of how long we must wait for our answer, we must not give up.

She is moved by her desperation into action. As a woman considered unclean, she had been sequestered in her home for 12 years. Yet she entered a crowd of people determined to see Jesus. The scripture in Matthew says she said to herself if I can just touch the hem of his garment I will be healed. That is what I call water walking faith.

She is moved by her faith to acknowledge that she was the person who touched Jesus. She made a declaration of faith. We all did that at one time in our lives. We came to know Jesus as our Savior and we made a statement of faith and suddenly we had a different direction.

And then Jesus called her "daughter," which let her know she was not only healed physically but she was healed spiritually, delivered from all that had almost killed her.

And the final thing we can learn from this woman is that she knew she had to be in the same proximity to Jesus to be healed. In other words, she had to be close enough to be able to touch His garment.

What about today? When we are desperate enough to receive a touch from Jesus, then we, too, will do whatever it takes to touch the hem of His garment. So how do we accomplish this? By getting built up in our most high faith through Bible reading, praying, being in a body of believers who will intercede for us, and by standing firm.

May we be willing to risk everything just to be near to our Lord.

In the name of the Father, and of the Son, and of the Holy Spirit. Amen.

The Parable of the Just

As children we learn to play fair, to share,
to expect right behavior to elicit right results.

The parables do not seem fair.

As young adults we model our lives after those
we respect, those we want to emulate.

The parables do not seem just.

We see the young man, inheritance squandered,
rewarded for his bad behavior.

Or was he?

We see the ninety-nine sheep abandoned
so that one could be found.

Or were they?

When we begin to see through Kingdom eyes
we will no longer look for justice, but

we will be thankful for mercy.

When we learn the meaning of discipleship
we will no longer complain that we are left behind

but we will journey with the Shepherd.

When we tear down the walls of prejudice

we will no longer be imprisoned by our own fear

but will find liberty and joy.

The parable of the just is a story of mercy,
the story of grace, of redemption sought

and redemption found.

Thanks be to God.

The Justice of God

Deuteronomy 32:1-4 (NIV)
1 Listen, you heavens, and I will speak; hear, you earth, the words of my mouth.
2 Let my teaching fall like rain and my words descend like dew, like showers on new grass, like abundant rain on tender plants.
3 I will proclaim the name of the Lord. Oh, praise the greatness of our God!
4 He is the Rock, his works are perfect, and all his ways are just.
A faithful God who does no wrong, upright and just is he.

Close to forty years ago, I picked up a rock from the bottom of the Buffalo River. It was a section of the river that was clear and shallow. I could see how the constant movement of the water reshaped the stone until it was round and smooth.

Do you know that the constant movement of God in your life can round out the rough edges and make your spirit smoother? I'm not saying that our lives will be carefree, but the Holy Spirit can take away the uneven edges of jealousy, unforgiveness, pettiness and pride, and when those qualities are washed away we will no longer cut ourselves and others on the jagged rock of our sinful nature.

In today's scripture, Moses is nearing the end of his life, and he is not just talking to God, he is talking to the heavens and the earth. He is proclaiming the greatness of God. When Moses referred to God as a rock, he was saying that God was strong, reliable, immovable and he went on to say that all of His works are perfect, and His ways are just.

Our Creator serves as the ultimate foundation for all integrity and justice. God's justice does not mimic man's justice. Man's justice is based on our idea that people should get what they deserve. God forbid. What we deserve is death because we are sinners, but God judges us in light of the redemptive work that Jesus did on Calvary. Where we deserve judgment, God chooses to give us mercy.

As Christ followers, may we always seek the justice of God over the justice of man. And rather than returning evil for evil, may we choose mercy over vengeance.

In the name of the Father, and of the Son, and of the Holy Spirit. Amen.

Time to Plant

Poetry grows from life,
and nature's law says
whatever you plant,
you harvest.

If you plant love, you
will reap love, but how
many of us think to spread
love's seeds into neat little
rows, watching over them
and tending to them, anxious
for the time when we see them
sprout from their place of
nourishment, to proliferate
and provide us sustenance
and keep us warm at night.

If you plant doubt and anxiety
you will not reap certainty and
assurance. The laws of poetry
are no different than the laws
of nature. Poetry grows
from what is planted. Plant
a few good words along the
way, hey?

A New Day

Micah 6:8 (NIV) He has told you, O mortal, what is good; and what does the LORD require of you but to do justice, and to love kindness, and to walk humbly with your God?

How can we strengthen our walk with God? Perhaps today provides the perfect opportunity to renew our commitment to love God with our heart, soul, mind and strength.

Micah was one of the minor prophets of the Old Testament. As you remember, being labeled a minor prophet was not because the work was less important than those labeled "major" prophets but was due to the smaller volume of work produced. But Micah's contribution was no less significant.

I have looked for justice for most of my seventy-three years, but I have to say the idea has been elusive. Yet this scripture calls out to me, beckoning me to treat others justly, or fairly, even if I am not treated that way myself. How do I accomplish such a goal?

Firstly, by remembering that treating others justly is a requirement of God. I like to remind myself, and others, that God's requirements are not suggestions. They are rules by which we should live.

Secondly, I acknowledge the fact that while man often lives according to what is right vs wrong, God's measure is good vs evil. What is the difference? Right and wrong are moral values that are subject to change based on culture and even the passage of time. Good and evil are spiritual values defined by God and are thus unchanging.

He has told you, oh man, what is good. May we today, and everyday, choose good.

In the name of the Father, and of the Son, and of the Holy Spirit. Amen

No More a Little White Lie

Taught not to lie, taught to
be honest, to act with
integrity, but only if
convenient, if the bottom
line is not affected, but
what effect will telling a
lie, teaching a lie, have
when training up a child
in the way he
should go?

Is there really any difference
between a little white lie and
a regular lie? Can a child
tell the difference?

Can you?

A Life of Balance

1 John 2:15-17 (ESV) Do not love the world or the things in the world. If anyone loves the world, the love of the Father is not in him. 16 For all that is in the world—the desires of the flesh and the desires of the eyes and pride in possessions—is not from the Father but is from the world. 17 And the world is passing away along with its desires, but whoever does the will of God abides forever.

When I was a child, I loved to ride the teeter-totter. But there was a problem. I was at least a head shorter and thirty pounds lighter than most of the other girls in my class, including my fraternal twin sister. So, in order to ride the teeter-totter, we had to compensate for my insufficiency. Either I would solicit another girl to ride with me to balance the rider on the other end, or I would have to sit as far back on the teeter-totter as was safe, and my sister would have to slide forward, which wasn't much fun for her.

Just as one must have balance in order to ride a teeter-totter, balance is needed in all aspects of life. Do we follow the Latin slogan Carpe Diem, seize the day, or should we follow a decidedly more spiritual path and adopt the slogan Soli deo Gloria, To God alone be glory? Do we have to choose between the two? Can't we have it both ways?

Jesus tells us in Matt 6:24 that no one can serve two masters, either he will hate the one and love the other or love the one and hate the other. But if we are not careful, we can become so heavenly minded we are of no earthly good. So, what is the answer? How do we find balance between the spiritual and the physical?

In John 17 Jesus says believers are in the world but not of the world. In the late 1700's song "Poor Wayfaring Stranger" we are told of the journey through this world toward a heavenly home where the traveller would be reunited with loved ones. "This World is not my Home" is another song that reminds us that, as believers, we have a future destination that supersedes our current home. First John reminds us that "desires of the eyes and pride in possessions" is not of God.

Somehow between the 1700's and the 21st century we have been transformed from pilgrims and strangers to becoming rooted in this world and the world system. We have become comfortable in our homes having more bathrooms than people, in our cars that cost more than many of our first homes, our boats, and even our planes. John Wesley, founder of Methodism, said, "I do not want to become so attached to my money that it goes to my heart."

Is that what has happened? Have we allowed our money and our possessions to make us so comfortable that we are holding tightly to what we have in this world and no longer looking forward to the life to come? Have we forsaken our duty not just to God but to God's people to care for those who cannot help themselves? As Paul would say, "God forbid."

May we turn our eyes upon Jesus, look full in His wonderful face.

In the name of the Father, and of the Son, and of the Holy Spirit. Amen.

The Lord is Countin' on You
By Stuart Hamblin

Go to the byways tell'em on the highways,
Tell them that you're their friend,
And tell'em the church is open,
They're welcome to drop in.

Talk just a little bit sing just a little bit,
Throw in a smile or two.
But heavy on the howdy doo,
For the Lord is counting on you.
Roy Rogers and Dale Evans recorded this song on their album "Jesus Loves You," 1960.

Come to the Table

Ps 23:5 (ESV) You prepare a table before me
in the presence of my enemies.
Luke 14:15-24 (ESV) 15 When one of those who reclined at table with him heard these things, he said to him, "Blessed is everyone who will eat bread in the kingdom of God!" 16 But he said to him, "A man once gave a great banquet and invited many. 17 And at the time for the banquet he sent his servant to say to those who had been invited, 'Come, for everything is now ready.' 18 But they all alike began to make excuses. The first said to him, 'I have bought a field, and I must go out and see it. Please have me excused.' 19 And another said, 'I have bought five yoke of oxen, and I go to examine them. Please have me excused.' 20 And another said, I have married a wife, and therefore I cannot come.' 21 So the servant came and reported these things to his master. Then the master of the house became angry and said to his servant, 'Go out quickly to the streets and lanes of the city, and bring in the poor and crippled and blind and lame.' 22 And the servant said, 'Sir, what you commanded has been done, and still there is room.' 23 And the master said to the servant, 'Go out to the highways and hedges and compel people to come in, that my house may be filled. 24 For I tell you, none of those men who were invited shall taste my banquet.'"

In the business world, when someone uses the phrase, come to the table, they are talking about negotiating a deal or a treaty. The invitation, or challenge, to come to the table is not about friendship—it is generally about who comes out on top.

In the kingdom world, the invitation to come to the table is issued by God Himself and it is about relationship, it is about putting God above all others. There is nothing to negotiate—Christ paid the price for our salvation, no strings attached. Either we accept His invitation or we miss the banquet.

When I think of coming to the table, the first thing that always comes to my mind is Psalm 23 where David tells us that God prepares a table for us in the presence of our enemies. David uses the analogy of a shepherd caring for his flock, and the shepherd seeks out the best pasture for feeding by going up to the high places. While the grass there is the sweetest, it is also a place of danger where lions and other animals of prey look for an opportunity to attack. But if the good shepherd invites us to the table, we should have no fear.

In the scripture from Luke, Jesus relates the story of a man who gave a great banquet. In the Middle East, being invited to eat with someone is a big deal. And as anyone who has ever prepared a thanksgiving meal is aware, you know the meal does not just come together. It takes weeks to prepare the menu, invite the guests—in Jesus' story even though the invited guests had plenty of notice of the banquet, and they had responded they would attend, when the day of the banquet came no one showed up.

The first person who declined to come said he had business to which to attend.
The second person said he had bought a herd of oxen, and he must tend them.
The third person said he had married and could not come.

So, the man throwing the banquet sent his servants out to the highways and byways, inviting the poor, the crippled, the blind and lame to come to the table. And do you know what happened? They came.

You see, what kept the originally invited guests from the table was not the reasons they gave. It was that they took their eyes off of the savior and let their business, their possessions and their families keep them away from God.

Perhaps the second group invited to the table had none of these distractions to keep them from God. Or perhaps they were so grateful to be invited that they would not let anything distract them—so the poor came as they were, the blind got someone to lead them, and the lame limped all the way to the table.

Dietrich Bonhoeffer was a German theologian who wrote about cheap grace. He said everyone wants grace, but contrasted cheap grace and costly grace: "Cheap grace is the grace we bestow on ourselves… the preaching of forgiveness without requiring repentance… grace without discipleship, grace without the cross, grace without Jesus Christ, living and incarnate… Costly grace is the gospel which must be sought again and again, the gift which must be asked for, the door at which a man must knock."

Jesus gave His life—there is nothing that we can add to what Jesus has already done.

The doors to the banquet hall will one day be closed. Come while the invitation is still open. Come.

In the name of the Father, and of the Son, and of the Holy Spirit. Amen.

Through a Child's Eyes

Amazing grace, extending
downward to a people who are lost.
Boundless love, unending
in its quest to embrace us at any cost.
Who is man that You are
mindful of him?
Who am I, why am I,
will I ever comprehend
the love that drew salvation's plan,
or the grace that restores
the heart of man.

Oh God, when I think
of your glory and majesty
I am humbled and in awe
that Jesus died for me.
But even more awesome than
His death upon that tree
is the resurrection power
that sets the captives free.

Thank God I am free.

Who is Jesus to You

John 1:1(NIV) In the beginning was the Word, and the Word was with God, and the Word was God. 2 He was with God in the beginning. 3 Through him all things were made; without him nothing was made that has been made. 4 In him was life, and that life was the light of all mankind. 5 The light shines in the darkness, and the darkness has not overcome it.

Have you ever thought of Jesus as being the Word, or do you only know Him as the babe in the manger about whom songs are sung and stories are told? If your Jesus is still in the manger and you take Him out only at Christmas, then you have not met the Jesus who came to set the captives free.

Or perhaps your Jesus is still displayed on the cross. Certainly, Jesus' sacrifice is a major aspect of who He is. After all, Jesus left the glory of heaven and was born to die so that we might live. But the Jesus on the Crucifix whom we meet only at Easter is not the Jesus we celebrate.

It is the resurrection Jesus from whom we receive the power to live, the power to defeat sin and ultimately death. It is the resurrection Jesus who gives us that old time religion. It is the Jesus who rose from the grave, defeated sin, death and hell, the Jesus who ascended to heaven to sit at the right hand of God the Father whom we must meet and make our dearest friend. And it is this same Jesus who left us not alone, but with the Holy Spirit, our comforter and the source of our spiritual power.

When we go back to John 1:1-5 we see that Jesus was actually the architect of the universe. It was Jesus who spoke the world into existence. It was Jesus who spoke the spark of life into all men. It was Jesus whose light extinguishes the darkness, for how can darkness exist if there is even the light from the head of a match. How much greater is the light that emanates from Jesus?

Holiness is not the same thing as righteousness. While righteousness becomes ours as a free gift, holiness is something we should pursue. Righteousness is a legal issue, but holiness is a character issue. Our righteousness, apart from Jesus, is as filthy rags, so we must put on the cloak of righteousness provided by Jesus Christ, and we must do it daily. Jesus' righteousness puts us in right standing with our Father.

Just as we have no righteousness of our own apart from Jesus, holiness is not a part of our character, but it is a part of God's character. We need righteousness to free us from death, but we need holiness to free us from life.

Salvation will always lead to righteousness, that is, right standing with God, but to live a righteous life before God takes something more--it requires holiness.

But is that possible? Everything God tells us to do can be achieved through the power of His spirit. If God tells us to do something, He has already made possible a way for it to be done.

God understands our limitations, but He can neither accept nor excuse them. Why? Because God is holy and He is just. May we seek after holiness today and every day.

In the name of the Father, and of the Son, and of the Holy Spirit. Amen.

Straight to the Heart

The Word of God, faithful and true,
able to stand alone, or
when blended with just the right notes,
just the right sounds,
travels over a keyboard,
or on strings, or upon the airy colors of a flute
and straight to the heart.

Sing with Gratitude

Col 3:12 (NIV) Therefore, as God's chosen people, holy and dearly loved, clothe yourselves with compassion, kindness, humility, gentleness and patience. 13 Bear with each other and forgive whatever grievances you may have against one another. Forgive as the Lord forgave you. 14 And over all these virtues put on love, which binds them all together in perfect unity.
15 Let the peace of Christ rule in your hearts, since as members of one body you were called to peace. And be thankful. 16 Let the word of Christ dwell in you richly as you teach and admonish one another with all wisdom, and as you sing psalms, hymns and spiritual songs with gratitude in your hearts to God. 17 And whatever you do, whether in word or deed, do it all in the name of the Lord Jesus, giving thanks to God the Father through him.

Many of us have enjoyed the musical version of Les Mis, the story of a man, Jean Valjean, who stole a loaf of bread and was sentenced to prison. Valjean became a hardened man while wearing the clothing of a prisoner. When he was released, his pardon came with a condition—he was to be considered a dangerous man, and as such no one would have anything to do with him.

Valjean received shelter in a monastery, but upon leaving repaid the kindness shown by stealing. He was still wearing the clothes of a guilty man. Yet, after the bishop spared him, Valjean examined his life and received forgiveness and redemption. He then exchanged his prison clothes for clothing befitting one who was redeemed. He lived out the remainder of his life helping others just as he had been helped.

Does our clothing reflect who we are? When we lived in Pittsburgh, we only had to drive around thirty miles to find at least some segments of an Amish community. Roadside stands selling jams can be found dotted around the rural areas, and lovely quilts are also easy to locate. The clothing of the "Plain People" stands out, and as hard as I tried to engage one of the clans in conversation, I was never successful.

Most Christians do not have a specific wardrobe that identifies us as followers of Christ. So how can people tell we are Christians? By our actions.

A popular song in the early '70's was "They Will Know We are Christians by Our Love", which expresses a sentiment we should try to adopt.

May we today, and every day, strive to reflect God's love in word and in deed. And may we "Sing the wondrous love of Jesus, sing His mercy and His grace."

In the name of the Father, and of the Son, and of the Holy Spirit. Amen.

The Journey Always Takes You Home

Think hope is gone, you
can't go on, the destination
too far, the road too hard?
Remember,
your journey will take you home.

Think life is unfair,
the scales broken beyond repair,
too late, nothing to remunerate?
Remember,
your journey will take you home.

Think bad times are all you know,
life's twists and turns left you
broken, too many dreams unspoken?
Remember,
your journey will take you home.

At the end of the day, you
will look back and say,
it's done, I was able to carry on.
I remembered,
my journey was only to take me home.

The Parable of the Prodigal

Luke 15:11-32 (NRSV)

11 Then Jesus said, "There was a man who had two sons. 12 The younger of them said to his father, 'Father, give me the share of the property that will belong to me.' So he divided his property between them. 13 A few days later the younger son gathered all he had and traveled to a distant country, and there he squandered his property in dissolute living. 14 When he had spent everything, a severe famine took place throughout that country, and he began to be in need. 15 So he went and hired himself out to one of the citizens of that country, who sent him to his fields to feed the pigs. 16 He would gladly have filled himself with the pods that the pigs were eating; and no one gave him anything. 17 But when he came to himself he said, 'How many of my father's hired hands have bread enough and to spare, but here I am dying of hunger! 18 I will get up and go to my father, and I will say to him, "Father, I have sinned against heaven and before you; 19 I am no longer worthy to be called your son; treat me like one of your hired hands."' 20 So he set off and went to his father. But while he was still far off, his father saw him and was filled with compassion; he ran and put his arms around him and kissed him. 21 Then the son said to him, 'Father, I have sinned against heaven and before you; I am no longer worthy to be called your son.' 22 But the father said to his slaves, 'Quickly, bring out a robe—the best one—and put it on him; put a ring on his finger and sandals on his feet. 23 And get the fatted calf and kill it and let us eat and celebrate; 24 for this son of mine was dead and is alive again; he was lost and is found!' And they began to celebrate.

Have you ever gone to a store or restaurant and asked for the Lost and Found. Usually, it consists of a cardboard box tucked away somewhere and everything that is lost is tossed unceremoniously into that box. You might find earphones, one glove, scarves, jackets, baseball caps, even cell phones. But no one would ever think to look for a person in the Lost and Found.

Thankfully, the father in our story did not need to seek out his lost son, because he returned of his own accord. As I read this parable over and over this week, I found some things that really stood out to me.

We all know the younger brother acted in rebellion towards his father. But do we understand the depth of his rebellion?

You see, by telling his father he wanted his inheritance now, it was the same as saying to his father, "I wish you were dead." And in order to generate the cash the son demanded, the father had to sell a portion of his land. There wasn't a First Bank of the Sons of the Parable from which the father could make a withdrawal. So, what was happening was not something that could be kept within the family—the entire community knew what was going on.

It did not matter that perhaps the father would need his hard-earned money before he died, nor that if his land had been left intact, it might have grown in value to become a great fortune. The father relented, and the scripture says he divided the property among the brothers.

And I'm thinking, Wimp, tell the kid he's not getting anything now and if he doesn't change his attitude, he won't get anything later. But you see, my version of the story would not have allowed for God's grace.

The younger son packed up and left the land of the Jews to travel to places where no one knew him, and he could do what he wanted. Picture this: Las Vegas of the Middle East, and what happens here, stays here. He spends all that he has on sex, booze and rock and roll, but a famine hits the land. Did you know that physical conditions in the Bible almost always parallel spiritual conditions. Not only was he bankrupt physically, but he was also bankrupt spiritually. Not only was he starving physically, but his spirit was also starving.

He ends up feeding the pigs of some local gentile—a Jew working for a gentile, feeding pigs which were considered unclean. How low he had descended, but that's what happens when we turn from our father, isn't it.

The son, half starved, comes to his senses and heads home. And I love this part. The father sees him coming from far away. Now I picture the father going out to the same spot day in, and day out, hoping to see his son coming home. And on this day that is exactly what happens.

The father is overjoyed and begins to run toward his son, which, in that culture, would have been a very undignified act. To prevent falling over his robe, the man would need to lift his garment, exposing his bare legs.

The father in the parable was willing to do whatever was necessary. He runs to his son, gladly restoring the young man, because that's what happens when we return to our father after living whatever way we choose. We repent, and we receive restoration.

Jesus shows us in this parable the character of God through the actions of the father. He is so loving, so forgiving, and he gives and keeps on giving. The father gives his younger son the finest robe that represents his standing in the family, a signet ring that represents authority, and shoes that represent his restoration to the family.

When the son returned, the father ran to him. If any of us has been living in Las Vegas, isn't it time to run back to the Father?

In the name of the Father, and of the Son, and of the Holy Spirit. Amen.

Reflections of a Life Well Spent

The waters of the pond are quiet now, and
my reflection is clear. It
was not always so, nor
will it always be. Storms leave
muddy waters.

I reach down, dragging my fingers
through the stillness, and see
the woman I was, and
the woman I've become. The
differences are clear. Believe it.
I see the answers are still fewer than
the questions, the reality
grimmer than the fantasy.
I see reflections of loss, I see
what each choice cost. I see
what time has done, and I know,
somehow, I just know, these
are reflections
of a life well spent.

Jonah, Jeremiah, and Habakkuk

Jonah 1:1-3 (NIV) The word of the LORD came to Jonah son of Amittai: 2 "Go to the great city of Nineveh and preach against it, because its wickedness has come up before me." 3 But Jonah ran away from the LORD and headed for Tarshish. He went down to Joppa, where he found a ship bound for that port. After paying the fare, he went aboard and sailed for Tarshish to flee from the LORD.

Lamentations 2 (NIV) 11 My eyes fail from weeping,
I am in torment within; my heart is poured out on the ground because my people are destroyed,

Hab 3:17-19 (NIV) 17 Though the fig tree does not bud
and there are no grapes on the vines, though the olive crop fails and the fields produce no food, though there are no sheep in the pen and no cattle in the stalls,18 yet I will rejoice in the LORD, I will be joyful in God my Savior. 19 The Sovereign LORD is my strength; he makes my feet like the feet of a deer, he enables me to tread on the heights.

Let's look for a moment at some of the minor prophets. When we read about Jeremiah, we see he is referred to as the weeping prophet. Habakkuk has been called the questioning prophet. But it seems to me that Jonah could be referred to as the angry prophet.

You see, God gave Jonah a prophecy some twenty years earlier, and then He was silent. But when God finally spoke again, it was a word Jonah did not want to deliver.

Why would God want Jonah to deliver a message of salvation to the Ninevites? They were a cruel people and Jonah was convinced if he carried God's word to them, they would repent and be saved.

So, Jonah ran. He ran down to Tarshish, down to Joppa, down to the hold of the ship, and ultimately he went down into the belly of the fish. The farther he ran from God, the deeper he descended into darkness. Sin does that.

But after three days Jonah was resurrected, a changed man. Or was he?

Jonah delivered God's word, and, as expected, the Ninevites repented and God relented. But rather than rejoicing, Jonah became so angry he threw himself a pity party.

Jeremiah was born into the tribe of Levi, and as such trained to be a priest. Yet at the age of nineteen, God told him he would be a prophet. He even told Jeremiah that this was His plan before Jeremiah was born. Jeremiah delivered God's word to the kingdom of Judah, and because of their wickedness, he cried.

Habakkuk delivered the message of God to Jerusalem and was forlorn because God would use the Babylonians to bring about their destruction. How could God use a people more wicked than they as an instrument of punishment?

Jeremiah wept, Habakkuk questioned, and Jonah gave in to his anger. Of these three men, I would rather emulate Habakkuk, who ultimately saw God for who He is and praised Him.

May each of us be delivered from the things that would separate us from the One, True and the Living God, and allow Him to lift us to the pinnacle of our faith.

In the name of the Father, and of the Son, and of the Holy Spirit. Amen.

Redeemed

To be saved, delivered, bought back, brought
back from the brink
of destruction, the edge of
oblivion,

but only if we remain teachable,
willing to listen
to others, readily yielding
to the Lord God.

If we cannot heed men, whom we
can see, then how
can we follow God, Who remains
wholly unseen.

A Tale of Two Men

Jonah 4:9 (NCV) But God said to Jonah, "Do you think it is right for you to be angry about the plant?"
Jonah answered, "It is right for me to be angry! I am so angry I could die!"
10 And the LORD said, "You are so concerned for that plant even though you did nothing to make it grow. It appeared one day, and the next day it died.
11 Then shouldn't I show concern for the great city Nineveh, which has more than one hundred twenty thousand people who do not know right from wrong, and many animals, too?"

Luke 15:28 (NCV) The older son was angry and would not go into the feast. So, his father went out and begged him to come in. 29 But the older son said to his father, 'I have served you like a slave for many years and have always obeyed your commands. But you never gave me even a young goat to have at a feast with my friends. 30 But your other son, who wasted all your money on prostitutes, comes home, and you kill the fat calf for him!' 31 The father said to him, 'Son, you are always with me, and all that I have is yours.'

Have you ever thought about the similarities between these two men and how their stories end? Both seemed to end abruptly, with less than a satisfactory resolution.

The first is the story of Jonah. Jonah had received a word to take to Ninevah, but refused. He ultimately relented, went to Ninevah, preached God's word, and, just as he feared, the

Ninevites were saved. For the story was never about Jonah or even the big fish, but the love, mercy and redeeming power of God.

Jonah was so angry he just sat under a tree. It was a tree God provided for shade, but just as suddenly as it appeared, it died. Jonah mourned the loss of the tree but refused to change his views of the Ninevites. And that is how the story ends, with Jonah consumed by anger.

The second story is about the prodigal son. Again, we all know the story, but have we noticed that there are two prodigal sons, not one? Even after the youngest son was restored to his father, the older son became separated from both his father and brother because of his anger over what he clearly perceived as favoritism.

Anger is listed among the acts of the flesh in Galatians 5. In some translations, instead of anger it reads "fits of rage." The "angerholic" is filled with righteous indignation, justifying every harsh word, every session of screaming, yelling and striking.

Life seems hopeless when faced with this behavior. But it is at the intersection of hopelessness and helplessness that God meets us. The stories of Jonah and the older brother ended with both men estranged from their families and from their God.

The best compliment I ever received was when I was told I was teachable. May we learn from these stories that God's faithfulness is great, but we must remain teachable, willing to learn and change, to avoid being part of another cautionary tale.

In the name of the Father, and of the Son, and of the Holy Spirit. Amen.

Seeing what Abraham saw

Obsidian sky dotted with astral bodies,
Jewel like in their beauty—
Can you count them,
Can you see them,
Can you see what Abraham saw?

Bush burns with lack of consumption,
Fire burns bright but no heat felt.
Can you see it,
Can you feel it,
Can you hear what Moses heard?

Sea separates the unholy from the Holy,
Gap is wide, too far to span.
Do you have faith
That covers the distance
Will you grab firmly the Savior's hand?
Will you?

The Majesty of God

Ps 19:1 (NIV) The heavens declare the glory of God; the skies proclaim the work of his hands. 2 Day after day they pour forth speech; night after night they reveal knowledge.
3 They have no speech, they use no words; no sound is heard from them.
4 Yet their voice goes out into all the earth, their words to the ends of the world.

I love seeing in the Scripture that nature itself declares God's glory. And David says that day and night the knowledge of the universe is revealed. To me that means continually! And listen to this—no speech, no sound, no words, yet their voice is not silent but travels to the ends of the earth. Powerful!

I am reminded of Jesus' entry into Jerusalem during His final week on Earth. The leaders feared the crowds were making so much noise that the Roman authorities would be notified, and the people would be punished. Jesus finally said, "Look, if the people stop praising my name, the very rocks will cry out." And in the letter to the Romans, Paul said all of creation shows the very glory of God.

Sometimes when I think of creation, my mind reflects on heaven and all that awaits us. I consider the wonders of heaven, but I do not dwell long upon the subject, because my imagination is not vivid enough to consider the beauty of heaven or the vastness of eternity. But when I look up at the night sky, particularly during those visits to places like Arizona where it seems as though you could reach up and grab a handful from the millions of stars, I am in awe. I wrote the poem "Seeing What Abraham Saw" during my first visit to the great southwestern United States. In a campground not far from the Grand Canyon, I stepped outside, looked up, and would have dropped to my knees if I had thought I could get back up.

That has been almost fifteen years ago, but this year, 2024, we had the excitement of watching a total eclipse of the sun from our very own yard. And in May the northern lights were visible in all fifty states. We couldn't see them here but the idea that many people in southern states could see them is incredible.

God's handiwork is all around us. May we today make the intentional choice to see God in His creation, and may His majesty sweep over our spirits, assuring us that the God Who created everything cares for us.

In the name of the Father, and of the Son, and of the Holy Spirit. Amen.

The Star-thrower

They call him the star-thrower.
He scours the beach in search of
that living organism more
shell than fish.
Gently he sends it spiraling
overhead. Then, just when it
seems it will never stop, it
begins its plummet to
the water's depths, the
life-sustaining, revitalizing
waters of the ocean from which
it came.

They call Him the star-thrower.
He scours the world in search of
that living organism more
spirit than flesh.
Gently he sends it spiraling
overhead. Then, just when it
seems it will never stop, it
begins its plummet to
the water's depths, the
life-sustaining, revitalizing
waters of the Holy Spirit from which
new life begins.

Knowing Jesus

(KJV) John 3:16 For God so loved the world, that he gave his only begotten Son, that whosoever believeth in him should not perish, but have everlasting life. 17 For God sent not his Son into the world to condemn the world; but that the world through him might be saved.
18 He that believeth on him is not condemned: but he that believeth not is condemned already, because he hath not believed in the name of the only begotten Son of God.

Knowing Jesus as your Savior is an act of faith brought about by grace. We were all dead in our sins, and it is only Jesus who can restore us to life.

What does it mean when we are restored to new life in Christ? It means we not only repent of our sins, we turn away from them. It means we become intentional in forming our lives to comply with the precepts of holiness found in God's Holy Word.

The prevenient grace provided by God before we even knew we needed it pulls us into a relationship with God. We are then justfied by grace and the salvation that comes only through grace begins to transform us.

Are you being transformed into the image of Christ? Do you see the world through Kingdom eyes or are you still trying to build your own mini kingdom, believing it is through your own efforts that you will achieve "happiness"?

Blessed are they who recognize the poverty of their spirits, and those who mourn over their sin nature. Blessed are the meek because they have turned control over to their God. Blessed are they who hunger and thirst after righteousness, or right standing with God. Blessed are the pure in heart, the transparent, who want only to love God more and to share that love with others. Blessed are they who shod their feet with the preparation of the gospel of peace. Blessed are they.

May we draw ever closer to Jesus, the healer of the brokenhearted, as we walk the pathway of righteousness.

In the name of the Father, and of the Son, and of the Holy Spirit. Amen.

I was there

Were you there when they
crucified
my Lord, just lyrics
to a song sung at Easter,
and not even my favorite
song.

But tonight, at yet another
Tenebrae,
I knew once and for all
I had to answer yes, yes
I was there, for it was my
sin

that nailed Him to the cross,
my sin
that caused Him to suffer
loss, the cost of humiliation
and death the price He had
to pay.

My sin proved impossible
to cover
in any way other than through
sacrifice of the most cruel kind,
redemption purchased with His
blood, not

mine. From one sinless, spotless,
and pure,
and now I no longer stand
accused, yet I can no longer
endure my part in the offering
only

He could provide, the Son of God
born to die
in my place, because God's grace
carved out a plan from the foundation
of the world to reconcile me to Him.

I was there.

The Resurrection of Jesus

John 20:1-20 (NRSV)
1 Early on the first day of the week, while it was still dark, Mary Magdalene came to the tomb and saw that the stone had been removed from the tomb. 2 So she ran and went to Simon Peter and the other disciple, the one whom Jesus loved, and said to them, "They have taken the Lord out of the tomb, and we do not know where they have laid him." 3 Then Peter and the other disciple set out and went toward the tomb. 4 The two were running together, but the other disciple outran Peter and reached the tomb first. 5 He bent down to look in and saw the linen wrappings lying there, but he did not go in. 6 Then Simon Peter came, following him, and went into the tomb. He saw the linen wrappings lying there, 7 and the cloth that had been on Jesus' head, not lying with the linen wrappings but rolled up in a place by itself. 8 Then the other disciple, who reached the tomb first, also went in, and he saw and believed; 9 for as yet they did not understand the scripture, that he must rise from the dead. 10 Then the disciples returned to their homes.

Jesus Appears to Mary Magdalene
11 But Mary stood weeping outside the tomb. As she wept, she bent over to look into the tomb; 12 and she saw two angels in white, sitting where the body of Jesus had been lying, one at the head and the other at the feet. 13 They said to her, "Woman, why are you weeping?" She said to them, "They have taken away my Lord, and I do not know where they have laid him." 14 When she had said this, she turned around and saw Jesus standing there, but she did not know that it was Jesus. 15 Jesus said to her, "Woman, why are you weeping? Whom

are you looking for?" Supposing him to be the gardener, she said to him, "Sir, if you have carried him away, tell me where you have laid him, and I will take him away." 16 Jesus said to her, "Mary!" She turned and said to him in Hebrew, "Rabbouni!" (which means Teacher). 17 Jesus said to her, "Do not hold on to me, because I have not yet ascended to the Father. But go to my brothers and say to them, 'I am ascending to my Father and your Father, to my God and your God.'" 18 Mary Magdalene went and announced to the disciples, "I have seen the Lord"; and she told them that he had said these things to her.

Jesus Appears to the Disciples

19 When it was evening on that day, the first day of the week, and the doors of the house where the disciples had met were locked for fear of the Jews, Jesus came and stood among them and said, "Peace be with you." 20 After he said this, he showed them his hands and his side. Then the disciples rejoiced when they saw the Lord.

I have always loved Easter. I love the dresses we wore as children, the patent leather shoes, dying Easter eggs, hunting eggs when I was a little girl and then hiding them when I had children. I love that we always woke up to baskets with chocolate and marshmallow rabbits, milk chocolate eggs, a stuffed toy. Even though we went to church on Easter, the best part of doing that as a child was wearing my new dress and new shoes. It would be a long time before the best part of Easter was knowing and understanding what Easter means to me as a Christian.

And when we go back and look at that first Easter, Jesus' disciples had no idea what Easter meant to them. Huddled together, they were heartbroken, they were frightened beyond belief. I doubt that any of us has ever experienced the same range of emotions during such a short period of time. Only one week earlier they had walked with Jesus into Jerusalem accompanied by cheering, the waving of palm branches, and they knew that the kingdom of God was at hand. What happened?

Very simply, the plan of salvation happened. The plan that our Bible tells us was in place from the foundation of the world happened. This Jesus whom they loved as a friend was now their risen Lord. What in the world do you do with that kind of information? Not only did the first disciples not know what to do, they were too frightened to do anything. The women had returned with the news of a miracle--a miracle of life, a miracle of hope. But it would be 50 days before the disciples had the courage to spread this message, 50 days before the Holy Spirit fell upon them at Pentecost. Then, they knew what to do with Easter.

The question for 21st century Christians is, "Now what? What comes next? What do we do with Easter?" We already have the power of the Holy Spirit residing within us so there is no reason to fear Easter. The truth is, we are Easter people. We were made for the resurrection and the life. But in order to experience resurrection we must first go through death. Death to self, death to this world, and ultimately death of this earthly body.

It is time for Easter people to join Job in saying, "I know that my Redeemer lives.' It is time for us to join Paul in saying "I want to know Christ and the power of His resurrection." As the Gaithers wrote, "Because He lives, I can face tomorrow, because He lives, all fear is gone, Because I know He holds the future and life is worth the living just because He lives."

In the name of the Father, and of the Son, and of the Holy Spirit. Amen

The Nature of Faith

Faith grows, or faith becomes less.
Faith is real, or it is not.
We were each given a measure of faith
and we are told "use it or lose it."

And so we do. We use our faith as
steppingstones, reaching
that higher ground that is
necessary for our Christian life.

A Faith More Precious than Gold

1 Peter 1:3 (NIV) Blessed be the God and Father of our Lord Jesus Christ! By his great mercy he has given us a new birth into a living hope through the resurrection of Jesus Christ from the dead, 4 and into an inheritance that is imperishable, undefiled, and unfading, kept in heaven for you, 5 who are being protected by the power of God through faith for a salvation ready to be revealed in the last time. 6 In this you rejoice, even if now for a little while you have had to suffer various trials, 7 so that the genuineness of your faith--being more precious than gold that, though perishable, is tested by fire--may be found to result in praise and glory and honor when Jesus Christ is revealed. 8 Although you have not seen him, you love him; and even though you do not see him now, you believe in him and rejoice with an indescribable and glorious joy, 9 for you are receiving the outcome of your faith, the salvation of your souls.

Today we move from the resurrection of Jesus to begin to examine our faith and discover what the resurrection means to us. You will remember that Peter was a fisherman from the fishing village of Capernaum on the Sea of Galilee. Peter was the brother of Andrew who had been a follower of John the Baptist. But when Jesus came on the scene, John pointed to Jesus and said to Andrew, there goes the son of God, and Andrew became the first apostle.

This letter is thought to have been written between 64 A.D. And 68 A.D. and was sent to people dispersed throughout parts of Asia. By this time there was great persecution of Christians, and Peter himself would be put to death by Nero around 68 A.D. So, this letter is one of encouragement to people who are already suffering because they are Christians.

The one thing that stood out to me as I was studying these verses was that Paul said the genuineness of their faith was more precious than gold, and that genuineness had been proven through the trials of suffering. Just as gold is tested and refined by the fire, faith is tested and refined by hardship.

When we compare faith to something as precious as gold, we find similar qualities. Just as gold is costly, so is our faith. While gold costs a great deal of money, genuine faith costs a great deal of endurance. We have people in our church who enjoy athletic endeavors, so you understand endurance. Endurance is remaining strong even in the face of opposition. If you are biking, the first time you face a hill you may not make it all of the way to the top, but each time you approach that hill you make more and more progress until finally you have reached the pinnacle. It is the same with our faith.

Just as gold is precious so is faith. When something is precious to us we treasure it. Some people put it in a box, others use it.

It is what I call the difference between mustard seed faith and water-walking faith. Why did Jesus use the mustard seed as an example of faith? When your faith is the size of a mustard seed, you plant it. Because when a mustard seed is planted and nurtured it grows into a strong tree.

You nourish your little faith with God's Word, you begin to rely upon that faith and your mustard seed faith begins to grow. But you don't take mustard seed faith and try to use it to walk upon the water. You need water walking faith to walk on the water. If you use mustard seed faith before it has grown sufficient for you to walk on the water, you will sink.

But here is something vital about faith. Eventually Jesus will say come because we were never meant to be confined in a little boat. We have to get out of the boat to exercise our faith, we have to get out of the boat to grow our faith, and we have to get out of the boat to share our faith.

Our scripture ends with Peter commending his audience by saying you believe even though you do not see, and you have received indescribable joy and the salvation of your souls. I read there was an inscription found on the basement walls of a house that was left in ruins during WWII.

I believe in the sun--even when it does not shine.
I believe in love--even when it is not shown.
I believe in God--even when He does not speak.

Can you say that you believe even though you have not seen? Do you have indescribable joy or have the waves of difficulty lapping at your feet caused your faith to waver and your joy to diminish?

May we allow our faith to grow because as we see God in action, our faith will necessarily get larger.

In the name of the Father, and of the Son, and of the Holy Spirit. Amen.

Developing Hind's Feet

I've been to the valley, so deep and so low
I thought I would never survive.
It seemed every problem and every foe,
joined forces to bury me alive.

I stayed in the valley, longer than needed,
and my time there was not well spent.
I moaned and I groaned about my lot in life,
and when I left it was without a hint

as to why I was sent there, or allowed to be there,
according to God's sovereign plan.
Had I gotten too big, when I should have stayed small,
was I unconcerned for my fellow man?

Or was it planned by the enemy to drive me to ruin,
thinking I would just give in?
Did he think the humiliation and pain in my heart
would really turn me towards him?

Did he think I'd forget the mercy of God
brought down by Jesus to man?
And how He had shed that mercy on me
even though I had sinned against Him.

No, I couldn't forget, so I began my climb
out of that valley so low.
It was a treacherous journey full of twists and turns
if I fell, there were only jagged rocks below.

I often stumbled but I never fell
for I was led by God's own hand.
He gently lifted me over the rough places
as I became conformed to the shape of His hand.

And with the high praises of God in my mouth
my problems and foes were defeated.
He had given me hind's feet to reach the high places,
my journey was almost completed.

I reached the high mountain, and looked at the valley
and saw what was there all the time.
A cross spans the distance and etched in that cross
are stairs to make easy the climb.

From the valley it's hidden, obscured by our woes,
it's only by Faith we can see.
But when we grab hold of that wonderful truth,
from satan's clutches we are finally free.

So I thank God for my valleys for they lead to the Cross,
and at the foot of the Cross Jesus meets me.
I give Him each burden, He gives me His grace,
so that nothing can ever defeat me.

The Call to Follow

Matthew 4:18 (NIV) As Jesus was walking beside the Sea of Galilee, he saw two brothers, Simon called Peter and his brother Andrew. They were casting a net into the lake, for they were fishermen. 19 "Come, follow me," Jesus said, "and I will send you out to fish for people." 20 At once they left their nets and followed him. 21 Going on from there, he saw two other brothers, James, son of Zebedee and his brother John. They were in a boat with their father Zebedee, preparing their nets. Jesus called them, 22 and immediately they left the boat and their father and followed him.

John 1:34 The next day John was there again with two of his disciples. When he saw Jesus passing by, he said, "Look, the Lamb of God!"

When the two disciples heard him say this, they followed Jesus. Turning around, Jesus saw them following and asked, "What do you want?"

They said, "Rabbi" (which means "Teacher"), "where are you staying?"

"Come," he replied, "and you will see."

Don't you love the way Jesus called the apostles to become a part of the gospel movement? Jesus went to where they were and called out "follow me" to these two men, Simon Peter and his brother James.

John's account shows how these two followers of John the Baptist left John and when they asked Jesus where He was going, Jesus simply replied, Come and see.

Jesus did not craft an elegant presentation to persuade men to follow Him. In fact, in Matt 8;20 Jesus tells people the son of man has no place to lay His head. Yet, the apostles followed. You see, the apostles did not just study a written text, they lived with the teacher, whose life was meant to be a living example of the Word.

Two thousand years have passed since Jesus left His place in heaven to become incarnate and He continues, through the Holy Spirit, to say to each of us "come and see." When we read the gospel accounts of Jesus' life and ministry, and when we allow His grace to penetrate our very being, then we, too, will answer the call to "come and see."

In the name of the Father, and of the Son and of the Holy Spirit. Amen.

Rise up

Rise up you people of faith,
rise up.
Hope is dimming but we're
not done yet.
Rise up.

Stand up you soldiers of the cross,
stand up.
The night is falling but
there is still time.
Stand up.

Kneel down you warriors of prayer,
kneel down.
Pray that hope, faith, belief
will all increase.
Kneel down.

Reach out, you disciples of Christ,
reach out.
There is still time to
spread the Word.
Reach out.

Join hands, you children of God,
join hands.
Let His light shine through you

that all might see Him.
Join hands.

Shine bright, you servants of God,
shine bright.
A single light pierces the darkness,
but millions of lights together overcome.
Shine bright.

Rise up, stand up, kneel down,
reach out,
join hands, shine bright.
You are here for a reason.
Rise up.

Intentional Discipleship

(NIV) John 13:34 "A new command I give you: Love one another. As I have loved you, so you must love one another. 35 By this everyone will know that you are my disciples, if you love one another."

When I was nine years old someone gave us an album by Roy Rogers and Dale Evans titled "Jesus Loves Me." One of the songs was "The Circuit Riding Preacher" and it included a poem by Edgar Guest. The poem, "Show Me" was revised as follows:

The Circuit Riding Preacher said these words one day,
I'd rather see a sermon than hear one any day,
and I'd rather one walk with me
than merely show the way.
For the best of all the preachers are the men who live their creeds
and to see their good in action
is what everybody needs.
Lord, I can learn to do it if they let me see it done,
I can watch their hands in action
but their tongues too fast may run.
And the sermons they deliver may be very wise and true
but I'd rather get my lesson by watching what they do.
For I may misunderstand them and the high advice they give,
but there's no misunderstanding how they act and how they live.

I loved this poem and tried to live it. I have to say I have not always been successful, but, again, I tried.

As a pastor I taught Wesley's Three Simple Rules: Do no harm, do good, and keep the ordinances of the Church. Simple, yes. Easy? Not always.

But we are never alone as we navigate this life. When Jesus left this mortal plane, he promised a Helper, or an Advocate, and so we have the Holy Spirit who empowers us to live according to the precepts found in the Holy Bible, embodied in the writings of John Wesley, and the creed found within this simple poem.

Today I encourage you to recommit your life to, as Ray Vander Laan says, "follow so closely to Jesus that the dust of His sandals covers you." May we determine not to settle for just being a Christian—be an intentional disciple.

In the name of the Father, and of the Son, and of the Holy Spirit. Amen.

Who is this God?

Who is this God we worship?
He is the God who set the stars
in space with only a word
because He is the Word.

Who is this God we praise?
He is the God who is the
wonder in wonderful
because He is YHWH.

Who is this God we serve?
He is the God who saved
us from our sins
because He loves us so.

Who is this God we follow?
He is the God who places
joy within our hearts
despite our circumstances.

Who is this God we emulate?
He is the God who is holy,
holy, holy, and we are expected
to be holy, holy, holy likewise.

Who is this God?
He is Jehovah T'sidkenu, our
righteousness. He is Jehovah
M'Kaddish who sets us apart.

Who is this God?
He is Jehovah Rophe, our
Shepherd, and he guides us
through the rough places.

Who is this God?
He is eternal, He is magnificent,
He is El Shaddai, the all-sufficient
One and our praise will never end.

The Importance of Hymns

Do you recall the first gospel hymn you ever memorized? I do. My twin sister and I memorized "The Old Rugged Cross" when we were nine years old. We had sung many hymns by that time in our young lives, but it was this song that grabbed our hearts and we sang it over and over while gently swaying on the front porch swing.

The Old Rugged Cross
By George Benard
On a hill far away stood an old rugged cross,
the emblem of suffering and shame.
And I love that old cross where the dearest and best,
for a world of lost sinners was slain.

So I'll cherish the old rugged cross (rugged cross)
till my trophies at last I lay down.
I will cling to the old rugged cross
and exchange it some day for a crown.

To the old rugged cross I will ever be true
its shame and reproach gladly bear.
Then he'll call me some day to my home far away
where his glory forever I'll share.

And I'll cherish the old rugged cross (rugged cross)
Till my trophies at last I lay down.
I will cling to the old rugged cross
and exchange it some day for a crown.

Music was always important in our family. Our grandparents sang songs like "Farther Along" and "The Lifeboat." We sat by our aunts in church and sang "Higher Ground" and "I'll Fly Away." There was something about those songs of our youth that just connected us with our God, and just as we learned these songs extolling the praises of our Creator and our Savior, we began to form our understanding of Who God was and who we were in Him.

And as we learned these great old hymns, we began to learn Scripture. At that time, the only translation of God's Word we had was the King James Bible, so to this day when I quote Scripture from memory it is from that translation.

As I grew older and my faith developed and strengthened, my soul was stirred over and over again by the songs of the church—Amazing Grace, How Great Thou Art, and Great is Thy Faithfulness. I find myself wondering, Are any of the songs so dear to me still heard by little girls today? Will they memorize these songs, leading them to memorize Holy Scripture?

I pray they do.

In the name of the Father, and of the Son, and of the Holy Spirit. Amen.

We're Only Human

Reconciliation, the act of restoration
of relationships between God
and man or between man and man.

We Christians are eager to accept
the regeneration that comes through
reconciliation to a Holy God,

but reconciling to our fellow man
is another matter as we fall back
on our humanity to excuse

our bad behavior, forgetting
or not caring that when Christ
reigns, sin should be reined in

and our humanity should be covered
by Christ's divinity. You think I am
trying to be perfect? No, not me.

But I do strive to live in obedience
to the command to be holy, the
demand that I love my neighbor

and I understand the requirement
to forgive, not because I feel like
it or another deserves it, but because

Jesus said do it. So, I seek holiness
knowing I will not be perfect,
but perfected in love, and that is

all I desire, all God requires.

Blessed is He who comes in the Name of the Lord

Matt 21:1 (NIV) As they approached Jerusalem and came to Bethphage on the Mount of Olives, Jesus sent two disciples, 2 saying to them, "Go to the village ahead of you, and at once you will find a donkey tied there, with her colt by her. Untie them and bring them to me. 3 If anyone says anything to you, say that the Lord needs them, and he will send them right away." 4 This took place to fulfill what was spoken through the prophet: 5 "Say to Daughter Zion, 'See, your king comes to you, gentle and riding on a donkey, and on a colt, the foal of a donkey.'"
6 The disciples went and did as Jesus had instructed them. 7 They brought the donkey and the colt and placed their cloaks on them for Jesus to sit on. 8 A very large crowd spread their cloaks on the road, while others cut branches from the trees and spread them on the road. 9 The crowds that went ahead of him and those that followed shouted, "Hosanna to the Son of David!"
"Blessed is he who comes in the name of the Lord!"
"Hosanna in the highest heaven!" 10 When Jesus entered Jerusalem, the whole city was stirred and asked, "Who is this?" 11 The crowds answered, "This is Jesus, the prophet from Nazareth in Galilee."

A little boy was ill and had to miss going to church on Palm Sunday. When his sister and father came home, they were carrying Palm leaves. "What's going on?" he wanted to know. The sister answered excitedly, "Jesus came and we waved these palm leaves over His head." The little boy stomped his foot and said, "Well that just figures. The one Sunday I miss and that's when Jesus decides to show up!"

I have to tell you, every Sunday, whether it is a special Sunday or just a regular Lord's Day, I always expect Jesus to show up. No one knew for sure if Jesus would come for Passover that year. Rumors were that the authorities wanted Jesus dead. Yet when Jesus passed by the excitement grew, and as the excitement grew, the noise swelled, and as the noise level grew, the crowd grew even larger.

I can imagine many of the people in the crowd that day wondered what was going on. Others began to tell the story of Lazarus and how Jesus preached the kingdom of God was at hand. And soon the word spread that the Messiah, prophesied from old, had finally arrived.

Many of those who gathered that first Palm Sunday to throw their coats and palm branches onto the street and who shouted praises did so because that was the way a king was treated. A carpet was rolled out for the king, returning from victory in war, who rode by in a carriage.

But some of the crowd had to be asking what kind of king was this? Why was he riding a donkey, which in the time of Jesus indicated he was coming in peace, instead of a magnificent steed, which meant war? Why did he look so meek? Where was the army he would use to overthrow the Roman government?

Yet they shouted out Hosanna, which meant 'save us.' Because Jesus had indeed come to save them, but the salvation He offered was the reconciliation of sinful man to a Holy God. And the man who rode a beast of burden into the city would soon be carrying our burdens upon his own back.

Freedom from Roman rule was never part of the plan.

Jesus did not come to meet our expectations or those of His fellow Jews. He came to meet our needs. He did not come to slay our enemies. He came to serve and give his life as a ransom for sin. For at its root, the real heart of the human dilemma is not our political problems, or our financial problems or even disease, but our sin sickness.

The road Jesus walked on Palm Sunday was the same road that would lead Him to calvary. The people shouting Hosanna that first Sunday, would be safely tucked in their beds when crowds stirred up by the authorities would cry out for his death in just a few days.

We might be tempted to wish Palm Sunday could have lasted forever, for this was Jesus' one moment where it seemed most people were ready to follow him. But Palm Sunday is not what brought salvation. Jesus had to continue down the road where he would ultimately pick up his cross, and we, too, as Disciples, must be willing to pick up our cross. Because, you see, Palm Sunday is not the defining point in Discipleship. The defining moment in Discipleship has always been, and will always be, the resurrection.

In the name of the Father, and of the Son, and of the Holy Spirit. Amen.

A Journey of Faith

Today we begin our Lenten journey
once again.
We leave behind the crisis of complacency,
the plethora
of poor choices, and walk the pathway
of reflection,
commitment, focusing on the cross,
always the cross.
For forty days we seek your face, pray
for your grace
knowing the trip is made sweeter
by what awaits
at the end of our journey of faith.

Letting Go

1 Sam 1:21 The man Elkanah and all his household went up to offer to the Lord the yearly sacrifice, and to pay his vow. 22 But Hannah did not go up, for she said to her husband, "As soon as the child is weaned, I will bring him, that he may appear in the presence of the Lord, and remain there forever; I will offer him as a nazirite for all time." 23 Her husband Elkanah said to her, "So what seems best to you, wait until you have weaned him; only—may the Lord establish his word." So the woman remained and nursed her son, until she weaned him. 24 When she had weaned him, she took him up with her, along with a three-year-old bull, an ephah of flour, and a skin of wine. She brought him to the house of the Lord at Shiloh; and the child was young. 25 Then they slaughtered the bull, and they brought the child to Eli. 26 And she said, "Oh, my lord! As you live, my lord, I am the woman who was standing here in your presence, praying to the Lord. 27 For this child I prayed; and the Lord has granted me the petition that I made to him. 28 Therefore I have lent him to the Lord; as long as he lives, he is given to the Lord."

Today's scripture deals with commitment, sacrifice and letting go. Hannah was barren, and in her culture other women ridiculed those who could not have children. So, Hannah went before the Lord and prayed that she might have a son, promised to dedicate that son to God's service, and then let go.

Now, for those of us who have had children, we have prayed similar prayers upon their births, thanking God and promising to raise our children according to His truths. But for Hannah, this prayer was more than a commitment; it was a sacrifice. After Hannah weaned her child, she took him and left him with the priest, Eli. Hannah made a commitment, then she made a sacrifice, and then she let go.

Each of our lives have included measures of commitment, sacrifice and even letting go. We have made commitments to spouses, to employers, and to churches. We have made sacrifices so that our children could have more than we had and so that they could be educated and able to live on their own. And we have each had much practice in letting go. Hannah let her child go at around age three, which to me is unimaginable.

I recall when I took my son, Jonathan, to kindergarten orientation. As they separated the parents from the children, my son ran to me, holding on to my leg and begging me not to leave him. Hard as it was, I had to let him go, but I knew I would get him back. When we drove Jonathan to college, his dad and I drove away, crying the whole three hours home. I had to let him go.

At this stage in our lives, we have become masters of letting go, yet each time we give something else up the pain of letting go resurfaces. A few years ago, there was a saying, "Let go and let God." It was a catchy saying, and certainly expressed an age-old truth. Instead of allowing God to be our co-pilot as the name in a popular book from a number of years ago expressed, we need to switch seats and ask Him to be our pilot. We have to let go of the controls and let God fly the plane.

As a licensed pilot we have procedures for transferring control of a plane. I would say, "You have the plane," and as I let go of the controls, the other pilot would respond, "I have the plane," taking the controls and the responsibility of the plane, and then one last time I would affirm, "You have the plane." If only letting go of anxieties and difficulties were as easy as saying, "God, you have my life," and then just let go.

Hannah did something few of us could ever do. She gave over her son, seeing him only one time per year as they brought their annual sacrifices, and she brought him a new robe. Can we learn from Hannah's story at this point in our lives?

May we make a fresh commitment to ask God to pilot us through the storms and difficulties of our lives, and then let go of the controls.

In the name of the Father, and of the Son, and of the Holy Spirit. Amen.

Turning Point

The moment when something changes,
incontrovertibly,
when life, or perspective, or both
does a 180 and you know
nothing

will ever be the
same again. That is
your turning point, your
defining moment
when you choose right or left

at Main Street
and the direction you choose
sets your course
for the rest of your life.

The turning point is when you need
a compass, a
method to find your way
home regardless of how far you have
roamed

or how lost you have
become.
Christ is your compass,
and the way home is through
the Cross.

Why? Because the loss
that brought
you to the foot of the Cross
also brings you to
the gates of glory.

And it is there you will find
peace.

Longing For God

Psalm 42:1 (NRSV) As a deer longs for flowing streams, so my soul longs for you, O God. 2 My soul thirsts for God, for the living God.

Ps 27(NRSV) 7 Hear, O LORD, when I cry aloud, be gracious to me and answer me! 8 "Come," my heart says, "seek his face!" Your face, LORD, do I seek.

I am in a season of my life where my longing for God is almost overwhelming. I seek out men and women who preach repentance, reconciliation and God's supernatural love. I listen to hymns that mirror the scriptures and even those praise and worships songs from the '70's and '80's that do the same. I spend more time not just reading the Word, but meditating upon the eternal truths found therein. I do all of this to draw nearer to God.

In my lifetime I have been in many Bible studies and I have taught many studies. I have taught Lenten studies and Advent studies. I have taught the parables and the beatitudes and taught two different studies on prayer. I have taught about the Rapture of the church and the Second Coming when Jesus establishes His kingdom on this earth.

I have taught about forgiveness using David and Saul as an example. I have taught about the trust exhibited by Gideon, and the faithfulness shown by Ruth when she left her home to accompany Naomi to Bethlehem.

When I read God's Word I begin by asking the Holy Spirit to allow me to understand the scripture in the same manner as those who wrote it. I pray that He keeps me from interjecting my prejudices and beliefs into the content so that the Word remains pure and untarnished by my human understanding.

And I revel in the Word being alive. I know this to be true because I never grow tired of the content. There is a familiarity in the stories, but at the same time there is a newness as God enlightens my understanding to new revelations that had previously been hidden.

So today as I read another passage it is with the expectation that I will continue to learn and be filled with the joy that comes from walking and talking with my Lord. And listening—always listening.

In the name of the Father, and of the Son and of the Holy Spirit. Amen

Rapture Ready

I'm rapture ready, heaven bound
but not until I hear that trumpet sound.
Until then we must watch and pray
and let our faith lead the way.

There are souls to save, mouths to feed,
we must go out and spread the seed
of love and kindness every day
for that, my friends, is the Wesleyan way.

The time is soon, whatever that means,
so we must not tarry or get caught up in routines.
For grace abounds and the Spirit leads
and salvation must be followed by our deeds

for faith without works is surely dead
and works without faith should fill us with dread.
So get ready with me to heed the call,
salvation and new life is available to all.

And the Angels Rejoiced

(NRSV) Luke 15:1 Now all the tax collectors and sinners were coming near to listen to him. 2 And the Pharisees and the scribes were grumbling and saying, "This fellow welcomes sinners and eats with them."
3 So he told them this parable: 4 "Which one of you, having a hundred sheep and losing one of them, does not leave the ninety-nine in the wilderness and go after the one that is lost until he finds it? 5 When he has found it, he lays it on his shoulders and rejoices. 6 And when he comes home, he calls together his friends and neighbors, saying to them, 'Rejoice with me, for I have found my sheep that was lost.' 7 Just so, I tell you, there will be more joy in heaven over one sinner who repents than over ninety-nine righteous persons who need no repentance.

Have you ever lost something that was precious to you and then found it? When I lived in Pittsburgh one of my friends there was my neighbor Candy. One day when she came over she realized she had lost her necklace. I looked in my house between sofa cushions and on the floor, but it was not there.

As we walked outside I saw something glimmering in the sun and bent down and it was Candy's necklace in the grass. She started crying and hugged me and it was only then that I realized just how much that necklace meant to her.

Today we are going to talk about one of my favorite parables, the parable of the lost sheep. The scripture begins with the

Pharisees upset yet again, this time because Jesus is in the presence of tax collectors and sinners. What was He thinking? If he was so holy, shouldn't He be hanging out with the holy people?

I can't help but think of Bugs Bunny and Elmer Fudd, and I want to say Silly Phawisees. When are you going to get it? And I want to reach back into time and shout to them, of course the sinners are drawn to Jesus. They are dying and they know it and He is the giver of life. If only you knew that you, too, are dying, then you could have new life as well.

So Jesus tells a series of three parables, each one dealing with something or someone who is lost.

The parable about the lost sheep has always been a little perplexing to me. From what I have read sheep are just plain dumb and helpless. If the shepherd does not keep their wool trimmed, it will grow so heavy that if they fall they cannot get back up but will lay there and die. Sheep will stand in the same spot and eat until the grass is bare, and not move on unless the shepherd guides them. They would rather drink stagnant, muddy water than drink from a brook because the bubbling of the water frightens them. If anyone or anything needs constant care, it is sheep.

But here is the part I don't understand. There are 100 sheep, and one wanders off. So, the shepherd leaves 99 defenseless sheep in the wilderness to go and search for one lost sheep. What if he can't find the lost sheep? What if he can't find his way back to the 99 sheep? Why didn't he just take the 99 sheep with him so that the flock would remain together. Why are these parables so hard to understand?

We need to look at some specifics in this illustration. First, Jesus is talking to people whose culture seems to have been black or white. Either you are holy like the Pharisees, or you are a sinner like the tax collectors. So, Jesus tells them about a shepherd who has lost a sheep—just one sheep. In Jewish society it did not matter how many sheep were safe, if a shepherd lost one sheep it would bring shame upon him. So, the Pharisees understood the need to find that lost sheep.

But did they understand that Jesus was trying to tell them a deep spiritual truth? We are so egocentric that we think everything, including our salvation, depends upon us. NO! That lost sheep did not try to find the shepherd, the shepherd searched for him. He did not rest until he found the sheep that had strayed. Likewise, when we are dead in our sins we do not seek out God, instead He seeks us out, and when He finds us, he holds us close to his heart, and when we repent there is much rejoicing.

But what about the 99? Didn't the shepherd risk their welfare by leaving them alone. I mean after all, they were good, God-fearing people, I mean sheep. They did everything right, but the shepherd didn't seem to care.

Instead, he has dinner with those who are lost and ignores the ones who are still together. Isn't the shepherd happy they have never been lost? Or are they lost? After all, they are in the wilderness.

If only the Pharisees could have seen that they were part of the 99 sheep, not safe in the shepherd's care, but in the wilderness of their sin, and in a way they were more lost than the sheep who had strayed. For when Jesus finds the one who is lost in his sin and he repents, there is rejoicing. But if we are not aware of our sin, then how can we repent?

It is a dilemma, isn't it?

Today we live in a world where sin has lost its meaning. Many of us live in the wilderness but we do not know it because there are so many other people there that it seems as though wilderness living is normal. Many of the people living in the wilderness are good people. But what we fail to understand is that good people die in their sins every day.

I saw a video clip recently about people approaching two men sitting at a table. As each person steps up to the table, he or she is carrying a file. The man at the table looks at the file and then the person steps on a scale. The scale measures the goodness or the badness of the person.

One after the other the scale reads "not good enough" and the person is sent to sit in another area. Then a man approaches and he has a really big file. But there is a stamp on the file and another man comes up to the table and says, "I have this." That other man is Jesus and He steps up on the scale and it reads "good enough."

There is nothing we can do that will make us good enough. Isaiah the prophet says our righteousness, our right standing with God, is as filthy rags. We are precious in God's sight, but we have no righteousness apart from Jesus. But when Jesus puts his stamp upon us, then we take on his righteousness and though we were lost, now we have been found.

If the wilderness looked dark and threatening, perhaps we would understand that without Jesus we are in trouble. But too often the wilderness looks like the place where we live, and we look like everybody else. It is only when Jesus pierces the darkness of our souls that we see we have been living in the wilderness, and then it is time to step into the light. And that is the good news.

In the name of the Father, and of the Son, and of the Holy Spirit. Amen.

Going Home (For Pa)

Went home one last time
to see the face of one I loved.
Once, full of vitality and life,
now a shell, empty and vacant
but free of earthly strife.
The spirit makes the man.

He loved family, fishing and friends,
and many loved him in return.
He saw good in all, though
not all were good;
a gift from God to show
the spirit makes the man.

Always ready with a joke, or
to lend a helping hand.
Ready to bring a laugh or a smile;
to keep peace and avoid conflict
he would go the extra mile.
The spirit makes the man.

Now he has gone home to
fish in the light of the Son.
We are saddened, but not forlorn,
for there will be a reunion
when our work on earth is done.
The spirit of God makes the man.

Life in the Spirit

Romans 8:1-8 (ESV)

1 There is therefore now no condemnation for those who are in Christ Jesus. 2 For the law of the Spirit of life has set you free in Christ Jesus from the law of sin and death. 3 For God has done what the law, weakened by the flesh, could not do. By sending his own Son in the likeness of sinful flesh and for sin, he condemned sin in the flesh, 4 in order that the righteous requirement of the law might be fulfilled in us, who walk not according to the flesh but according to the Spirit. 5 For those who live according to the flesh set their minds on the things of the flesh, but those who live according to the Spirit set their minds on the things of the Spirit. 6 For to set the mind on the flesh is death, but to set the mind on the Spirit is life and peace. 7 For the mind that is set on the flesh is hostile to God, for it does not submit to God's law; indeed, it cannot. 8 Those who are in the flesh cannot please God.

Years ago there was a late-night program called "Soap" which was a parody of daytime soap operas. There were many eccentric characters on this show, one of whom was played by Katherine Helmond. I don't remember a lot about the show, but I recall there was a storyline where Helmond was being set up for murder, and as the police carried her away, she kept repeating, but I'm innocent, I'm innocent.

For those of us who are not lawyers, it is interesting to note that the term innocent is not the same as the term not guilty.

Not guilty is a legal term which means the evidence presented was insufficient to find a person guilty of charges. The best example I can think of is OJ Simpson, who was found not guilty of murdering his wife and a young man. But we would be hard pressed to find many people who believe a not guilty verdict meant Simpson was innocent. So, I thought today we could look into what it means for Christians to be not guilty of their sins because of the blood of Jesus.

The first verse in today's scripture is a familiar one: there is no condemnation for those who are in Christ Jesus. Sometimes it seems we do not understand the full implication of this verse.

There is a struggle between our flesh and our spirits, so when we look at today's scripture it is so reassuring to see that condemnation has been lifted. Why? Not because of anything we have done but because of what Jesus did for us. And because we are no longer condemned, we can live in hope and not despair.

When I think of despair I think of Job and all that he suffered. We don't know how long Satan was able to attack Job, but we do know it was at least a period of months. Most of us find it almost impossible to endure illnesses that only last for days, and yet Job was able to hold strong. His friends accused him of doing something to cause his own problems, his wife told him to curse God and die, yet Job clung to God and God's word. Why?

Because he knew who God was. He uttered the words, the Lord giveth and He taketh away, because he trusted God completely. When we really get to know God, we begin to understand God's character and when we take the time to learn who God is, then when God tells us because of Jesus Christ we are no longer condemned, we can believe it.

Does the lifting of condemnation mean we will no longer struggle with temptation. No, but it means we will not struggle in vain because we do not struggle alone. We have the Holy Spirit as our advocate and we have our church family who will stand in the gap for us, interceding when the walls that keep us from giving in to sin begin to crumble. We have Jesus Christ who sits at the right hand of God forever intervening on our behalf. That should be good news to everyone.

In today's world, some tend to live as Christians only on Sunday, but Christ crucified sin so that we can reject a lifestyle of sin and live according to the spirit every day of the week. And so we live as everyday Christians, not just when others are watching, but are transformed by his word and his love because that is the desire of our hearts.

Our scripture ends by saying those who are in the flesh cannot please God. What is it about us that prevents us from wanting to please God? Don't children want to please their parents? Then why shouldn't we want to please our Heavenly Father? He's not expecting perfection, but he does desire our devotion. Devotion is more than loyalty. Devotion is an act where we consecrate our lives to him. Think he expects too much?

Aren't you thankful God did not think it was too much to let His Son die so that we might live? Aren't you thankful that Jesus willingly gave Himself up for us that we could be free? Aren't you thankful the Holy Spirit brought Jesus out of the grave so that He might live and that same Holy Spirit lives within us and will raise us up into eternal life?

You see, as intentional disciples, we have been given the great gift of being able to walk in the light of His truth. The truth is that even though we are not innocent of our sins, because of Jesus we are no longer guilty. Because of Jesus, we can live in freedom, because of Jesus we can walk in love, because of Jesus we live in faith, and because of Jesus we have a hope that never fails.

When we reach the time when each of us stands before that Great White Throne of Judgment, I do not expect God to judge me innocent of anything I have done on this earth. But I do expect to hear him say that Jesus Christ has already pled my case, paid the price, and I have been found not guilty.

In the name of the Father, and of the Son, and of the Holy Spirit. Amen.

A Mother's Heart

The mother sat beside the bed
where her daughter lay.
The doctor said the child
would not live another day.

The mother fell upon her knees
and began to fervently pray,
"Dear God, please heal my baby,
don't take her, let her stay."

The mother stayed, the mother prayed
late into the night.
But when she saw death's shadow
she knew she had lost the fight.

"Take me instead, and let her live,
my life is as good as done.
I cannot bear to let her go,
her life has just begun."

"I am not the monster people fear,"
she heard death softly say.
"I am an angel sent by God
to take your child the rest of the way.

Look at the face of the one you love,
she is not afraid to go.
Nor will you be when your time arrives
for the Father loves you so.

Your precious child completed
all God intended her to do.
Her place now is in heaven
where she will wait for you."

The room grew quiet, the air was still
as she felt her daughter go.
She held her hand and touched her face
and said, "I love you so.

Go be with God, we'll be fine here,
don't worry, fret or cry.
We will all be together again
in the blinking of an eye.

You are in my heart forever,
nothing can ever take your place."
Then she bowed her head and prayed to God,
"Dear Lord, I need your grace."

God heard her prayer and began to send
friends and loved ones, too.
She was overwhelmed with kindness
as she saw God's love shining through

each act of love, each spoken word,
each sweet and tender caress.
And in the midst of life's greatest sorrow,
a mother felt eternally blessed.

A Steadfast Love

Ruth 1:14 (KJV) And they lifted up their voice, and wept again: and Orpah kissed her mother-in-law; but Ruth clave unto her. 15 And she said, Behold, thy sister-in-law is gone back unto her people, and unto her gods: return thou after thy sister-in-law. 16 And Ruth said, Intreat me not to leave thee, or to return from following after thee: for whither thou goest, I will go; and where thou lodgest, I will lodge: thy people shall be my people, and thy God my God: 17 Where thou diest, will I die, and there will I be buried: the LORD do so to me, and more also, if ought but death part thee and me.

Steadfast love—Having a loyal and firm love. The love exhibited in the book of Ruth is beyond most mortal love.
You know the story. Naomi and her husband leave Jerusalem during a severe famine and travel into Moab, where her sons meet and marry Moabite women.

Naomi's husband and two sons die, leaving her in a foreign land with her daughters-in-law. (It is important to remember that women in that culture were completely dependent upon their husbands, unable to own property or make a living.) Totally bereft, Naomi tells her sons' wives to return to their mothers and she will return to her homeland.

But Ruth, with a love and devotion that exceeds anything many of us can understand, clings to her mother-in-law. She leaves the only land she has ever known, working in the fields to reap the corn and grain left intentionally according to Levitical Law to supply for those who had no provisions. This law, found in Leviticus 19:9-10 and referred to as gleaning, was a divine obligation of landowners and considered a fruit of holiness.

The rest of the story shows us how Boaz, the owner of the field, becomes the Kinsman Redeemer of Naomi and Ruth and is ultimately the ancestor of King David. Ruth becomes one of only two Gentiles in the bloodline of Jesus.

I delivered a sermon a few years ago called "The Steadfast Love of God" and the final point was that we can never outrun the love of God, nor out sin the mercy of God.

Just as Ruth gives us a snapshot of a deep sacrificial love, God shows us the truest love of all. "For God so loved the world, He gave His only begotten Son, that whosoever believes in Him shall not perish but have everlasting life." John 3:16

May we know, understand, and believe that Jesus is our Kinsman Redeemer and His steadfast love will save us.

In the name of the Father, and of the Son and of the Holy Spirit. Amen.

WHAT IS PRAYER?

Prayer is communion with God. God desires our fellowship, but we require time spent with Him.

Prayer includes the following elements:
communion, adoration, thanksgiving, confession, petition, intercession, submission. We should not do all of the talking in prayer. When we pray the Scripture, God is faithful to speak to us.

WHAT PRAYER ISN'T

Prayer is not presenting God with a wish list and then sitting back and letting Him go to work.

Prayer is not a weapon we use against our enemies, where we beseech God to afflict those who hurt us with scourges and plagues. Such prayers are called "imprecatory" and while there are instances in the Psalms of David praying in this manner, I cannot imagine doing so.

Prayer is not where we turn as a matter of last resort, nor is it a bargaining tool where we promise God we'll do something if He does something in return.

When we take God's name in vain, or speak it foolishly, that is not prayer.

When we tell someone we'll pray for them, and then don't, our intention, regardless of how good it may be, is not prayer.

When we join in corporate prayer but then find our minds wandering, then we have left the prayer realm and entered the imagination realm (2 Cor 10:5).

THINGS THAT HINDER OUR PRAYERS

There are certain things that will hinder our prayers, and we need to be careful to avoid them. The Bible lists some as follows:
Insincere prayer--Is 1:15-20
Showy prayers--Matt 6:5
Not being clear-minded & self-controlled--1 Pet 4:7
Acts of the sinful nature--Gal 5:19-21

Prayer and Bible reading are the two methods where our humanity meets God's Divinity.

May we draw close to God as we seek Him out in His Word and through prayer.

In the name of the Father, and of the Son, and of the Holy Spirit. Amen.

The Gap

The Gap, a place for young men's clothing
In the '90's, but not quite the
same gap one stands in.

You know the one—the
hole in the wall where those
wanting nothing more than

to wreak havoc on the Hebrews
rebuilding the wall around Jerusalem
could sneak through

under cover of darkness.

But there they were—kneeling, praying,
standing in the gap, and so
here we are today,
kneeling, praying, standing in the gap.

Standing in the Gap

(NIV) Neh 4: 12 Then the Jews who lived near them came and told us ten times over, "Wherever you turn, they will attack us." 13 Therefore I stationed some of the people behind the lowest points of the wall at the exposed places, posting them by families, with their swords, spears and bows. 14 After I looked things over, I stood up and said to the nobles, the officials and the rest of the people, "Don't be afraid of them. Remember the Lord, who is great and awesome, and fight for your families, your sons and your daughters, your wives and your homes."

It has been years since I heard anyone use the phrase "standing in the gap," which is another way of describing intercessory prayer. When we approach God on behalf of someone else, we are interceding for that precious soul. Just as Nehemiah stationed people armed with spears to stand in the gaps in the wall surrounding Jerusalem so that the rebuilding of that structure could continue, we are commissioned to keep the enemy at bay with our prayers so that our brothers and sisters in Christ can be victorious.

What tools do we need to intervene for someone else? We arm ourselves not with spears but with the preparation of the gospel of peace as found in Eph 6:10. We put on the helmet of salvation which protects our minds from thoughts that would bring us down. We put on the breastplate of righteousness which protects our heart. We have no righteousness in and of ourselves, but through Jesus Christ we are made whole.

We put the belt of truth around our waist, we pick up the shield of faith and the sword we use is the very word of God. And, this last piece of equipment is vital—we put on the shoes of peace so that wherever we walk we leave footprints of tranquility.

It is then, and only then, that we are ready to stand in the gap.

I leave you with one final thought. When you pledge to pray for someone, you have made a sacred vow. Don't allow distractions to keep you from fulfilling your commitment. Be strong in the Lord and be of good courage. And know, believe and understand that your prayers make a difference.

In the name of the Father, and of the Son and of the Holy Spirit. Amen.

They Just Sang Praises

When Paul and Silas were in that old jail,
beaten and bruised, it seemed all hope had failed.
But Paul said to Silas, in spite of everything,
sometimes you just have to sing.

You just sing praises, praises
when life gets you down, you just have to stand
and sing praises, praises,
praises to the Great I Am.

Singing in the Storm

In case you're wondering, this is not the Gene Kelly, Debbie Reynolds "Singin' in the Rain" kind of singing. This is the Paul and Silas sitting in a cold, dark jail cell kind of singing.

Ps 71:23 My lips will shout for joy when I sing praise to you--I, whom you have redeemed.

Ps 126: 2 Our mouths were filled with laughter, our tongues with songs of joy. Then it was said among the nations, "The LORD has done great things for them."
3 The LORD has done great things for us, and we are filled with joy. 4 Restore our fortunes, O LORD, like streams in the Negev. 5 Those who sow in tears
will reap with songs of joy. 6 He who goes out weeping, carrying seed to sow, will return with songs of joy, carrying sheaves with him."

I know of no person who enjoys being in the midst of a storm, especially me. When we are in a storm, whether physical or spiritual, we look first for a means of escape, and barring that, we look for shelter.

But although storms can be devastatingly destructive, they can do two things: they can reveal your character, and they can produce a godly character within you.

In the book of Jonah, the sailors who threw Jonah overboard to save themselves revealed themselves to be men of faith, but they were faithful to the wrong God. In fact, Jonah 1:4 said all the men were afraid of the storm and each called out to his own god. Through the casting of lots, God revealed that Jonah was the reason the storm had befallen the ship. Jonah then instructed the other sailors to throw him overboard and the storm would cease. The sailors did not want to do this, for fear that Jonah's death would then be on their heads, but they finally conceded, after first praying to Jonah's God for forgiveness and mercy.

Jonah was revealed to be a man who recognized his responsibility and bore the consequences of his actions. Jonah made a bad choice by running from God, and bad choices produce bad results.

After the sailors threw Jonah overboard, they immediately offered sacrifices to God and made vows to Him. While we do not know the nature of these vows, it is clear new character was produced in these men. Where before they feared what the storm would do to them, now they feared, or were in awe of, God--not the pagan gods they had previously worshipped, but the One, True and Living God.

Jonah learned one thing during this encounter: he learned that to be used of God, one must have a heart for God's people. Sadly, although he went on to carry God's message to the Ninevites, his story ends with him angry at God and likely never used by God again.

Do you tend to shake your fists in anger towards God during the midst of a storm, or do you bow down on your knees, thanking God for His safekeeping thus far? It matters less whether the storms were sent by Satan to crush you, or God to test you, than what your reaction is to the storm.

In the midst of the storm, why not try turning to Scripture? Read Ps 27, Ps 91 by, Is 55:12, Jer 29:11, and Rom 8:28 for encouragement. (Try looking at these scriptures in an Amplified Bible for added benefit.)

Singing praises to God in times of difficulty not only produces joy in the singer, but it is also a witness of God's faithfulness to all who hear. Read Acts 16 for the account of Paul and Silas singing in the jail!

"1 Thess 5:16 Be joyful always;17 pray continually; 18 give thanks in all circumstances, for this is God's will for you in Christ Jesus."

Joy is a habit. If you work at maintaining your joy in all circumstances, and practice praying continually, it is much easier to thank God in any situation that arises. Practice may not always make perfect, but it does make it easier to rely on prayer and have a spirit of joy when your habits have led to a prayerful, joyful lifestyle.

In the name of the Father, and of the Son, and of the Holy Spirit. Amen.

And Then There is Hope

Zephaniah 3:17 The LORD your God is in your midst, a mighty one who will save; he will rejoice over you with gladness; he will quiet you by his love; he will exult over you with loud singing.

Romans 5:2-5 Through him we have also obtained access by faith into this grace in which we stand, and we rejoice in hope of the glory of God. More than that, we rejoice in our sufferings, knowing that suffering produces endurance, and endurance produces character, and character produces hope, and hope does not put us to shame, because God's love has been poured into our hearts through the Holy Spirit who has been given to us.

Psalm 25:4-6 Guide me in your truth and teach me, for you are God my Savior, and my hope is in you all day long.

Jeremiah 29:11 For I know the plans I have for you," declares the LORD, "plans to prosper you and not to harm you, plans to give you hope and a future."

Psalm 31:24 Be strong and take heart, all you who hope in the LORD.

Proverbs 23:18 There is surely a future hope for you, and your hope will not be cut off.

Hebrews 10:22 let us draw near to God with a sincere heart in full assurance of faith, having our hearts sprinkled to cleanse us from a guilty conscience and having our bodies washed with pure water. 23 Let us hold unswervingly to the hope we profess, for he who promised is faithful. 24 And let us consider how we may spur one another on toward love and good deeds.

Hebrews 11: 1 Now faith is being sure of what we hope for and certain of what we do not see. 2 This is what the ancients were commended for.

Hope is that innate quality born into each one of us. As children our hopes are necessarily child-like. We "hope" the Tooth Fairy will leave some coins under our pillow and we "hope" we will get the presents we want for our birthday and Christmas.

But as we grow older our hopes change. We may go through periods where we hope we have enough money to make it until the next payday. Or perhaps we hope we will get the promotion for which we have waited and believe we deserve.

As Christians our hope is in the God of our salvation, the Mighty One of Israel, our Rock and our Defender. Hope fans the fires of faith, and faith strengthens our belief.

Keep faith alive by spending time with your Heavenly Father, recognizing that He wants only the best for you.
When life takes its toll on you, turn to God, the Author and Finisher of your faith. Time spent in prayer is never wasted. Tell Him of your needs, thank Him for all He has done in the past, and praise Him for who He is and what He is getting ready to do for you.

In the name of the Father, and of the Son, and of the Holy Spirit. Amen.

Hope

Hope drifts in on angel's wings, barely
disturbing the air, the room, we
hardly know it's there.
Yet, it arrives, unhurried, but
not unwanted.
We see it in the
face of a friend, the
trace of a smile, or simply
a kind word. It is the promise
of good things to come, the
assurance that we are not alone. It is
what gets us through another day
when we think we cannot go on.

The Red Thread
A story of Faith, Obedience, Redemption, Deliverance

Joshua 2:1 Then Joshua son of Nun secretly sent two spies from Shittim. "Go, look over the land," he said, "especially Jericho." So, they went and entered the house of a prostitute named Rahab and stayed there.
2 The king of Jericho was told, "Look! Some of the Israelites have come here tonight to spy out the land." 3 So the king of Jericho sent this message to Rahab: "Bring out the men who came to you and entered your house, because they have come to spy out the whole land."
4 But the woman had taken the two men and hidden them. She said, "Yes, the men came to me, but I did not know where they had come from. 5 At dusk, when it was time to close the city gate, the men left. I don't know which way they went. Go after them quickly. You may catch up with them." 6 (But she had taken them up to the roof and hidden them under the stalks of flax she had laid out on the roof.) 7 So the men set out in pursuit of the spies on the road that leads to the fords of the Jordan, and as soon as the pursuers had gone out, the gate was shut.

When we think of how God has worked to bring about His kingdom, we often have trouble seeing ourselves as part of His mighty plan. We might find ourselves thinking "if only I were more like David, or Peter, or Paul, then God could use me." But what we tend to forget is that throughout history, God has used flawed and blemished individuals, just like David, Peter and Paul, to bring about His purpose and fulfill His plans. And, individuals just like us.

About Rahab:
1. A Gentile
2. A prostitute
3. Heard of the God of Israel and repented
4. Bold enough to defy the king and bargain with representatives of Joshua
5. One of the four women mentioned in Jesus' bloodline
6. Rahab heard of the One, True and Living God and believed
7. Rahab acted on her belief
8. Rahab trusted God to protect her

HEB 11:1 Now faith is being sure of what we hope for and certain of what we do not see.

Rahab was told to hang a scarlet cord from her window, so that she and all of her family would be saved. How fitting that a scarlet cord was used, a symbol of the blood of the Passover lamb, as well as the ultimate Lamb of redemption.

When Rahab hung that scarlet cord from the window, she was hanging her faith out of the window for all to see. Her faith, just like the scarlet cord, stood out, it was noticeable, it didn't blend in with those around her.

When you decide to hang your faith out of the window, you will no longer blend in with many of the people around you. You will be noticed. But just remember, you will also be delivered.

Faith, obedience, redemption and deliverance--can you see how one leads to the other? The steppingstone of faith leads to the obedience of the cross, and at the foot of the cross we find redemption, which then sets us on the pathway to deliverance.

In the name of the Father, and of the Son, and of the Holy Spirit. Amen.

Bring them in, Build them up, Send them out

Bring them in, the hurting, the lost,
those who need healing
and salvation.

Give them a place where they can be
transformed by the saving grace
of Jesus Christ,

where they can be at long last free

from the sin that ruled their life,
free from the chains that kept
them bound.

Build them up, those who have been
justified by grace through faith
in Jesus Christ

and see how disciples grow.

Send them out, those who are being
sanctified daily, perfected in the love
of God

so that they can show that same love
to all they encounter along
life's way.

Bring them in, build them up, send them out in the name of Jesus, through the power of the Holy Spirit,

and according to God's command.

Come and see...Go and Tell

John 1:35-39

(NRSV) 35 The next day John again was standing with two of his disciples, 36 and as he watched Jesus walk by, he exclaimed, "Look, here is the Lamb of God!" 37 The two disciples heard him say this, and they followed Jesus. 38 When Jesus turned and saw them following, he said to them, "What are you looking for?" They said to him, "Rabbi" (which translated means Teacher), "where are you staying?" 39 He said to them, "Come and see."

(NRSV) Matthew 28:18 And Jesus came and said to them, "All authority in heaven and on earth has been given to me. 19 Go therefore and make disciples of all nations, baptizing them in the name of the Father and of the Son and of the Holy Spirit, 20 and teaching them to obey everything that I have commanded you. And remember, I am with you always, to the end of the age."

I have always been intrigued by ellipses, you know, those three little dots that I used in the sermon title. Ellipses are a device used to omit the fluff in writing and get down to the basics. When used to begin a sentence, we know that something has occurred before—maybe we should check it out. When ellipses are used to end a sentence, we know that the story is not yet over, something more is going to happen.

But today I used ellipses in the middle of my sermon title which might indicate I am omitting 3 1/2 years of Jesus' teaching, His life, His work on this earth. What's up with that? As Paul would say, God forbid! Today it means simply that I would like for us to focus on two things—the call and the mission, the invitation to come and the commandment to go.

Jesus began to call His disciples immediately after returning from 40 days in the wilderness. The custom in those days was for students to choose their rabbi, their teacher, and so when John the Baptist pointed to Jesus and said, that is the Lamb of God, two of John's followers immediately left John and began to follow Jesus. Some might think John would have been hurt by this seeming lack of loyalty. Not so. John the Baptist knew his role in history—in His-story, and John had served as a signpost, but Jesus was the Way.

So, two men, Andrew and his brother Simon Peter followed Jesus. Their plan was to see which home he entered, go and knock on the door, and if he invited them in, that signaled he was agreeing to be their teacher. But Jesus turned and said, "What are you looking for?"

The disciples were possibly caught by surprise, and instead of answering, we want to be your disciples, they said, we want to know where you are staying. Jesus answered, come and see. What a simple yet compelling invitation.

Jesus could have said, it's the third house on the left with the thatched roof. You can't miss it. But give me an hour to tidy up first. No, he said Come and see—it was an immediate and genuine invitation. See who God really is, because when you see me, you will have seen the Father. Come and see and you will know, believe and understand that the promises made by the prophets are being fulfilled right before your eyes.

But they learned that very day if you want to be intentional in your discipleship, you need to come and stay because the only way you can truly know Jesus is to abide with Him.

I would call your attention to the sunflower whose blooms will either follow the track of the sun, or at the least will face east. What if we as disciples of Jesus Christ had a true transformation of heart and life and we became Son-flowers with our faces so firmly fixed on Jesus that we would only follow the Son.

And that's exactly what the first Disciples did. They stayed and then they did what disciples do...they told others to come and see. Because they were filled with joy unspeakable and full of glory. They had been in the presence of Jesus the Christ, and nothing was ever going to be the same. And the disciples came, one after another, to come and see, come take His yoke upon themselves, to come and drink of the living waters, and to come and rest.

People often wonder what God's will is for us individually. Some of us have a distinct call to preach, to teach, to care for others. But we have all been called to go ye therefore into all the world to preach the gospel of Jesus Christ. But preacher, he can't be talking to me. I can't speak. Neither could Moses. I'm too small. Gideon was in the smallest tribe of Israel and yet he answered God's call. David knocked down a giant.

We must remember that "Go" is a command, not a suggestion. And, we are not going under our own authority but the authority of Jesus and the power of the Holy Spirit. And we must never forget disciples are made by teaching, by showing, so we don't just go and tell, we go and make disciples.

This is exactly what these first disciples did. They began to proclaim the gospel of Jesus Christ, that mystery of how God sent His son, His only son, to bring salvation to a people who were lost in their sins, to restore lost and dying man into fellowship with God, and to reveal that God was going to do a new thing—he was grafting a new branch into the vine for the gentiles.

So how do we make disciples? Our churches are our command centers. Within these walls we have people who are hurting and so we try to help them heal. We have folks who teach, and those who come to be taught. We have some whose ministry is here in the church, while for others their ministry begins after they exit the church on Sunday morning.

But one of the primary reasons for being in church, apart from praising and worshipping God, is to make disciples. We bring people in; we love them and care for them. Then we build them up in their most high faith by teaching the Bible; we pray, and then we send them out.

We find ways we can help in the community. Having a heat wave? Then find out who is suffering and buy fans for them. Are there hungry people around you? Feed them. I will tell you not many people that you help will show up for church, but you have been a disciple when you have helped the least of these.

"Come and see" is where your journey with Christ begins, "go and tell" is where the journey takes you. Do both.

In the name of the Father, and of the Son, and of the Holy Spirit. Amen.

Build Yourself Up

Jude 1:17-23 (NRSV) 17 But you, beloved, must remember the predictions of the apostles of our Lord Jesus Christ; 18 for they said to you, "In the last time there will be scoffers, indulging their own ungodly lusts." 19 It is these worldly people, devoid of the Spirit, who are causing divisions. 20 But you, beloved, build yourselves up on your most holy faith; pray in the Holy Spirit; 21 keep yourselves in the love of God; look forward to the mercy of our Lord Jesus Christ that leads to eternal life. 22 And have mercy on some who are wavering; 23 save others by snatching them out of the fire; and have mercy on still others with fear, hating even the tunic defiled by their bodies.

Jude, identified as the brother of James the Just, probably wrote this epistle around 60 A.D. The purpose of this letter was to encourage believers to stand fast in the faith, not allowing false teachers to undermine the gospel of Jesus Christ.

Do you suppose the writers of the New Testament had the hope that their writing, inspired and empowered by the Holy Spirit, would put an end to falsehoods surrounding the gospel? I would imagine that was certainly their goal.

Yet today false teachers abound, some of them emerging from our seminaries, teaching that the Bible is archaic, casting doubt on many of the writers of the Scriptures, and telling those of us who still hold the Bible as cherished that we are worshipping the Bible rather than the God of the Bible. Really?

The Holy Bible is God's revelation of Who He is, and each book carries the theme of redemption. God has revealed Himself to us through the Scriptures, through His Son, and through nature itself. If we cannot believe the Bible, then it is not a matter of the Bible being wrong or out of touch with today's culture, it goes strictly to the heart of faith.

If we do not have confidence (faith) in the Bible, then how do we maintain our belief and relationship with the God of the Bible? How do we allow Jesus to be our personal Savior and Lord if we separate Him from the Bible? After all, everything we know of Jesus comes from the Bible. We are even told in John 1 that Jesus is the Word made flesh.

If you find yourself under the teaching that says the Bible is not for today, or someone who picks and chooses from the Scripture those words that make him or her comfortable, run. Instead of trying to receive inspiration from one who is devoid of the spirit of God, learn to do as Jude says and build yourself up in your most high faith.

Stay in the Word and be sure you are reading an authorized translation and not a paraphrase of the Bible. What is the difference? A translation works directly from the Hebrew and Greek and translates into English (or your native tongue) the best words and meaning of God's Word. It is a word for word study, or a thought for thought study, that gives us the closest meaning to the original text. A paraphrase takes paragraphs or segments of the word and tries to make it more understandable, often in today's language.

Fill your spirit not just with the Word, but with hymns and songs extolling God and His Son. Let your spirit soar as you listen to or join in to sing those songs that lift up God in praise. Pray, pray, pray like there is no tomorrow, because brothers and sisters, we do not know how long we have on this earth. But however long we are here, we must align ourselves with the Truth, and that Truth can only be found by learning and adhering to the WHOLE Word of God.

May we allow the Spirit of the Most High God to fill us to overflowing, and may we then share what we have received with others.

In the name of the Father, and of the Son, and of the Holy Spirit. Amen.

For Such a Time as This

Events orchestrated, coincidences
occur, that leave us
scratching our heads in wonder,
reeling from the thunder
of what could have been, what should
have been another ill defeat,
yet God was in the details
and the victory was sweet
because He raised up another
warrior, for such a time as this,
and again we saw His saving
grace and knew nothing was amiss.

God is raising up warriors
all across the land,
mighty in His strength
but how can they withstand
the march of satan's army,
growing day by day,
and the hopelessness and futility
that seem to darken our way.
Even many churches
have floundered and gone to sleep
while God's children are beaten and bruised
and thrown upon the heap.

God is raising up warriors
for such a time as this,

when we must rely upon the One
with the nail holes in His wrist.
Can you hear Jesus calling
your name out loud and clear,
can you step out from the shadows
and throw off the cloak of fear?
Many will be chosen
but only some will heed the call
to follow the Master where he leads,
to willingly give their all.

Perhaps you have been chosen,
for such a time as this.

Get Ready!

(NIV) Est 4:13 "Do not think that because you are in the king's house you alone of all the Jews will escape. 14 For if you remain silent at this time, relief and deliverance for the Jews will arise from another place, but you and your father's family will perish. And who knows but that you have come to your royal position for such a time as this?

This is the story of Esther. Esther was a Jew, the cousin of Mordecai but taken in by him as his goddaughter. Esther was her Persian name, for like others during the Diaspora, she was renamed. Her Jewish name was Hadassah. Mordecai, the uncle or cousin, was clearly Jewish, and he did not hide his heritage, but Esther did not make her heritage known.

The book of Esther was almost not included in the Bible because there is not one mention of God in the entire book. There is a mention of fasting, and the institution of the Festival of Purim, but again, God is not referenced.

One of the King's top men was Haman and he was infuriated when Mordecai, a known Jew, would not bow down before him. So he issued a decree in the king's name to have all of the Jews killed. Notice in the scripture that Mordecai tore his clothing, covered himself with ashes and paraded up and down the street, stopping short of entering the king's gates.

The scripture mentions fasting. It could be that many of the Jews had forsaken their worship of God, but once they were faced, yet again, with the threat of extinction, they began fasting and weeping. When I hear of someone fasting and weeping, I immediately think they are communicating with God both in contrition and with intentionality.

As we read the book of Esther, we find she had heard nothing of the decree to kill the Jews, nor that Haman was the perpetrator of this scheme. But now Mordecai was asking Esther to do the impossible. She would be exposing herself as a Jew. She would have to go before the king without being summoned by him, which was punishable by death.

For such a time as this---I love that. Mordecai says if you do not do this, deliverance will come from another place. Throughout the Jewish history, God always put people into place to save the Jews from extinction. Esther is now a part of the Jewish community and willing to die so that they might live.

Esther was right where God wanted her to be. How do you know you are where God wants you to be?

You will not have to fight your battles alone=Gideon
You will be content whatever your situation=Paul
You are making a difference=Nehemiah
God's grace is sufficient=Shadrach, Meschach, and Abednego
Your faith is strengthened despite adversity=Isaac

Perhaps you have been chosen for such a time as this. There is one thing of which we can be sure: God's plans will not be thwarted. If you do not answer His call, someone else will. So when God calls, answer with a resounding, "Here am I, Lord."

In the name of the Father, and of the Son and of the Holy Spirit. Amen.

Blessed Are They

Blessed are the poor in spirit, theirs
is the kingdom of heaven.
Blessed are they who mourn for
comfort shall be given.
I know this something you've not heard before
that's why I tell you myself
Blessed are they who heed my words, blessed are they.

Changing our Attitude

Matthew 5:1 (NRSV) When Jesus saw the crowds, he went up the mountain; and after he sat down, his disciples came to him. 2 Then he began to speak, and taught them, saying: 3 "Blessed are the poor in spirit, for theirs is the kingdom of heaven. 4 "Blessed are those who mourn, for they will be comforted."

Don't you love the fifth chapter of Matthew? I always say that John is my favorite gospel, but then there is Matthew 5. Where else can we find such an abundance of kingdom understanding? So, let us delve into these particular lessons for the comfort found there.

I love, love, love the beatitudes. The way Jesus uses the first blessing as the foundation for all that follows is brilliant. The fact that we must recognize the poverty of our own spirit before we can draw close to God encourages us to put our faith under a microscope, and by doing so we can then, and only then, begin our spiritual journey toward salvation and, ultimately, holiness.

Years ago my brother and I shared an apartment. He was in college, and I was in a low paying job. We went grocery shopping, and I carefully selected the items needed, knowing how little I had in my checking account. To my surprise and dismay, even after carefully selecting only the items we needed, the total was more than I had.

Just before we started putting things back, I asked the lady at the cash register to recheck the groceries. She was annoyed, but upon doing so she found she had charged $10 more for the milk than the actual price.

Although we were able to buy our groceries, the knowledge that I was so low on funds was like a punch in the stomach. It almost took my breath away. Likewise, when we realize how close to poverty our spiritual account is, we should be brought to the same reaction.

In Isaac Watt's song "At the Cross" the first stanza reads:

"Alas! and did my Savior bleed, And did my Sovereign die? Would he devote that sacred Head For such a worm as I?"
The lyrics penned by Isaac Watts in 1707 reveals a stark change in the way we think of our self worth. The phrase "for such a worm as I" has become so abhorrent that it was replaced with "sinners such as I" and then revised again to read "someone such as I."

Really? Have we become so proud that we are blind to our sin nature? The idea that God would not only allow His Son to die for sinful mankind, but indeed, that was God's plan from the foundation of the world, is almost incomprehensible, yet that is exactly what happened.

And what is our reward when confronted with our poverty in spirit? Jesus does not promise that the kingdom of heaven will be our future reward. No, He says the kingdom of heaven is ours now. Praise God!

I am convinced that when God looks at me, He does not see my sin because it is covered by the blood of Jesus. When I put on the cloak of righteousness each morning as I start my new day, I am declaring "I will not be separated from God today because of my sin nature. I will come into His presence and He will accept me as His own." If I am to be holy, I must be able not only to wear the coat of righteousness myself, I must be willing to share that coat with others. When I begin to see others as God sees them, I will know that I am becoming conformed to His likeness and I am attaining holiness.

When we finally comprehend that we are completely bankrupt in our spirit, that knowledge should necessarily turn into mourning, a deep anguish that only God can heal. We will then be in a position to repent of our sins and turn toward Jesus. Then we will receive the supernatural comfort that only comes from God.

So, be blessed, be happy, receive now the kingdom promised by Jesus.

In the name of the Father, and of the Son, and of the Holy Spirit. Amen

Living by Faith

It takes faith to make it through the day
Faith to carry you all the way
Just live as God tells you to
And never ask why.

There are times when you won't understand
But just hold fast to his hand
And He'll lead you through the valley
To the land of eternal day.

Hope In the Lord

Lam 3:22 (NRSV) The steadfast love of the LORD never ceases, his mercies never come to an end. 23 they are new every morning; great is your faithfulness. 24 "The LORD is my portion," says my soul, "therefore I will hope in him."

If you have known me long, you realize that hope is a recurring theme in my writing. So why would I read Lamentations if I am seeking hope?

I read Lamentations because it is one of the sixty six books of the Bible and, as Paul said in his letter to Timothy (NRSV) 2 Tim 3:16 "All scripture is inspired by God and is useful for teaching, for reproof, for correction, and for training in righteousness." Therefore, I include all of the Bible in my studies.

Lamentations is not an easy book to read. We find the prophet Jeremiah walking through the remains of his beloved Jerusalem, once a vibrant city, but now desolate and in ruins.

Earlier, in the book of Jeremiah, we see a young man called by God to proclaim His word to a people who had turned their backs on God. Jeremiah is known as "the weeping prophet" because the message he had to deliver was truly almost more than he could bear.

During Jeremiah's formative years, he was in training to be a priest having been born into the tribe of Levi. When God called him to be a prophet instead, Jeremiah protested, but ultimately acquiesced. It is during Jeremiah's lament over Jerusalem that he acknowledges God's love and faithfulness.

I am thankful for the words of the prophet who spent so much of his life literally weeping over the separation of his people from God, but who could also proclaim that God's love was steadfast and new every morning.

May we, today and everyday, take a moment to find our hope in the God whose "mercies are new every morning."

In the name of the Father, and of the Son and of the Holy Spirit. Amen

Hope, pray, believe

Hope is a gift
straight from the heart
of God.
Hope drives us to sit
by the bedside of a loved one
in the darkest of nights
even when the doctor
says no hope exists.

Prayer is God's promise
that He is only a whisper
away.
Prayer connects us to
our Creator, our Savior, and
it both forms and informs us.
Prayer gives voice to hope,
and is the foundation for belief.

Belief is the ability
to see as reality
those things
only imagined. Hope
drives us to prayer, and prayer
is carried to the throne of God
on the back of belief
by wings of faith.

Hope, pray, believe...
more than a slogan,
it is a way of life.
Hope, Pray, Believe…

Grace offers hope, and hope leads to peace

Jeremiah 29:11
"For I know the plans I have for you," says the Lord. "They are plans for good and not for disaster, to give you a future and a hope."

Psalm 94:19 When doubts filled my mind, your comfort gave me renewed hope and cheer.

Romans 5:2-5
Through him we have also obtained access by faith into this grace in which we stand, and we rejoice in hope of the glory of God. More than that, we rejoice in our sufferings, knowing that suffering produces endurance, and endurance produces character, and character produces hope, and hope does not put us to shame, because God's love has been poured into our hearts through the Holy Spirit who has been given to us.

Romans 15:13
May the God of hope fill you with all joy and peace in believing, so that by the power of the Holy Spirit you may abound in hope.

Hebrews 11:1
Now faith is the assurance of things hoped for, the conviction of things not seen.

Hope is not the opposite of faith, but instead hope leads to and strengthens our faith. Hope in God is not some magic formula or a wish or even a desire. Hope in God is the confidence we have that God is ever near and that he always wants the best for his children.

After having my first book published, I wrestled with what inscription to include with my signature, and I came up with Hope, Pray, Believe. To me this simple phrase reflects as well as anything the foundation of my belief system.

My hope is in the Lord my God and in Jesus His only son, who lived, died and was resurrected all for me. And because I have placed my hope in Him, I pray to Him with confidence, knowing that if He does not give me what I want, He will always give me what I need.

Prayer is that communication that I can have with the Most High God, a time of quiet, a time of meditation where God both informs my understanding and forms my character. Our scripture today says that though everything fails, we should rejoice in the Lord.

I love the word "rejoice," because its root word is joy, and joy is one of the fruits of the spirit. As Christians we should exhibit the fruits of the spirit in all we say and do.
The fruits of the spirit are love, joy, peace, forbearance, kindness, goodness, faithfulness, gentleness and self-control. Why is it important that we bear these fruits? Because the fruit is the visible proof of what is in the tree and the fruits of the spirit are the visible proofs of what is in the heart.

Belief is the acceptance of a truth, and our truth is the gospel of Jesus Christ. The Amplified Bible says belief is when we trust in, adhere to and rely upon such truth. Don't you love that? Our belief in Jesus goes deeper than just accepting what someone else has told us or acknowledging He is the son of God. Belief forms a platform whereby we stand firm on God's Word and hold fast to faith. Hope, Pray, Believe. It is all about God.

In the name of the Father, and of the Son, and of the Holy Spirit. Amen

The Big Picture

Seeing only what is visible
With the naked eye.
The moon, absent its craters,
The stars, covering the sky,

But God, who cradles the whole world
In His hands and in His heart
Sees from horizon to horizon
And knows the story from finish to start.

Yet I Will Rejoice

Habakkuk 3:17-19
17 Though the fig tree does not bud
 and there are no grapes on the vines,
though the olive crop fails
 and the fields produce no food,
though there are no sheep in the pen
 and no cattle in the stalls,
18 yet I will rejoice in the Lord,
 I will be joyful in God my Savior.
19 The Sovereign Lord is my strength;
 he makes my feet like the feet of a deer,
 he enables me to go on the heights.

One of my favorite books is "Hinds Feet on High Places" by Hannah Hurnard. In this book we meet the Fearings who live in the Valley of Humiliation. The main character is Much-Afraid, one who has physical infirmities and is so fearful that she can hardly leave her cottage. But the Good Shepherd has promised her salvation if she will follow him.

Escaping her relatives, she follows the Shepherd, who assigns her two companions to help her along the way, but much to her dismay her helpers are Sorrow and Suffering. This reminds me of the song from Hee Haw:

Gloom, despair, agony on me,
deep dark depression excessive misery.
If it weren't for bad luck I'd have no luck at all
Gloom, despair, agony on me.

Thankfully after much tribulation Much Afraid is transformed and her companions change from being Sorrow and Suffering to Grace and Glory.

Habakkuk, the questioning prophet, spent years questioning God. But the above scripture reflects his ultimate understanding of who God is.

May we remember that we can not see the big picture, but our God is all-knowing. Let us turn to Him, in faith, continually praising Him for who He is, and waiting to see what He is going to do next.

In the name of the Father, and of the Son, and of the Holy Spirit. Amen

The Gospel of Peace

I love the Word. The Word of God,
Scripture made flesh,
flesh made into sacrifice
for my redemption and yours.

When I feel the fabric of the carpet
against my knees, I know
I am reaching out and touching
Someone not just greater than I,

but someone who loves more,
cares more, gives more grace,
shows more mercy
than I ever will.

If I could only keep my feet shod with
the preparation of the gospel of peace
all of my waking hours,
then I would leave footprints

of peace wherever I go.
Then, I, too, would care more,
grace more, and mercy more
than I ever have before.

Perfect Peace

John 11:20 (NIV) When Martha heard that Jesus was coming, she went to meet Him, while Mary remained sitting in the house. 21 Martha then said to Jesus, Master, if You had been here, my brother would not have died. 22 And even now I know that whatever You ask from God, He will grant it to You. 23 Jesus said to her, Your brother shall rise again. 24 Martha replied, I know that he will rise again in the resurrection at the last day. 25 Jesus said to her, I am [Myself] the Resurrection and the Life. Whoever believes in (adheres to, trusts in, and relies on) Me, although he may die, yet he shall live; 26 And whoever continues to live and believes in (has faith in, cleaves to, and relies on) Me shall never [actually] die at all. Do you believe this? 27 She said to Him, Yes, Lord, I have believed [I do believe] that You are the Christ (the Messiah, the Anointed One), the Son of God, [even He] Who was to come into the world. [It is for Your coming that the world has waited.] 28 After she had said this, she went back and called her sister Mary, privately whispering to her, The Teacher is close at hand and is asking for you. 29 When she heard this, she sprang up quickly and went to Him. 30 Now Jesus had not yet entered the village but was still at the same spot where Martha had met Him. 31 When the Jews who were sitting with her in the house and consoling her saw how hastily Mary had arisen and gone out, they followed her, supposing that she was going to the tomb to pour out her grief there. 32 When Mary came to the place where Jesus was and saw Him, she dropped down at His feet, saying to Him, Lord, if You had been here, my brother would not have died. 33 When Jesus saw her sobbing, and the Jews who came with

her [also] sobbing, He was deeply moved in spirit and troubled. [He chafed in spirit and sighed and was disturbed.] 34 And He said, Where have you laid him? They said to Him, Lord, come and see.
35 Jesus wept.

When someone dies, we often hear "it was God's will." Yet, we see in this passage that Jesus was not only distressed by Lazarus' death to the point of weeping, verse 33 says he was deeply moved and troubled. Jesus saw first hand the hold that death has upon us, and He was gaining a glimpse into how His own death would affect His followers.

And notice how, when Jesus asked where Lazarus was buried, the sisters replied, "Come and see," the very same phrase Jesus used in calling the disciples. The grace that God showered on each of us through the death and resurrection of His Son offers the hope that those who believe in Jesus will live, and that hope leads to a peace that passes all human understanding.

And the peace of God, which transcends all understanding, will guard your hearts and your minds in Christ Jesus. Phil 4:7

You will keep in perfect peace him whose mind is steadfast, because he trusts in you. Isaiah 26:3

In the name of the Father, and of the Son, and of the Holy Spirit. Amen.

Seeking Peace

(NKJV) Heb 12:14 Pursue peace with all people, and holiness, without which no one will see the Lord: 15 looking carefully lest anyone fall short of the grace of God; lest any root of bitterness springing up cause trouble, and by this many become defiled;

I normally focus on love and joy, but with so much unrest in the world I began to wonder about the root of such chaos. Surely the lack of peace begins early—it does not spring forth full grown.

We have all known people who cannot live in peace. Generally such a person literally seethes with anger. There is no reasoning with such an individual, and their justification is "you shouldn't have made me so mad."

I find myself wondering what would have happened if, upon first displaying such unreasonable hostility, the parents had quashed the temper tantrum of their small child. Would that person have learned to live in peace rather than create chaos?

The scripture says we are to pursue peace. In other words, peace does not just happen, we have to seek after peace.

And did you know we are to put on holiness? Since we have no righteousness, or right standing with God, apart from what we receive through Jesus, it is necessary for us to put on the garments of holiness.

If our anger provokes us to fits of temper and even rage, then we are not pursuing peace or holiness, without which no one will see God. The scripture goes on to say if we do not seek peace a root of bitterness can spring up, through which many will be defiled. You see, it is not just the person displaying such fits of anger that is damaged, but those subject to repeated assaults can become bitter and resentful.

May we go before God each day, seeking the strength to live according to His good will. If we are angry, may God give us a spirit of peace and reconciliation. And if we are resentful, may God give us a spirit of forgiveness.

In the name of the Father, and of the Son, and of the Holy Spirit. Amen.

What Would Happen?

What would happen
if we were given
a way to escape
all the way to heaven, a
means to evade
the cares of this
world, wings that would
suddenly become unfurled,
and carry us to places
yet untold, places where
we could finally be bold, and
leave behind the woes of today,
tomorrow's sorrows still far away, and
even the words that would
burn a hole into the
essence of our souls
would be left behind, their
damage yet undone, while
we searched to find our
place in the sun.

Would we be happy, or at least
free, or would we be
tethered still for eternity
to life's battles, waging them one
by one, until we're bruised and scarred,
tired and alone, but not undone.

Humble Yourself

(NIV) 1 Peter 5:6 Humble yourselves, therefore, under God's mighty hand, that he may lift you up in due time. 7 Cast all your anxiety on him because he cares for you.

It seems that people today find nothing wrong with pride. Yet, God calls for us to humble ourselves, so what are we to do?

To attain humility, we must draw closer to God. If we desire a closer relationship with God, we must begin with meditating on the Word. I like to read the Word aloud, because something happens when words are vocalized—they seem to take on a life of their own.

When we practice humility, we are accepting that God is great, while we are small. We are acknowledging that our worth is found in who we are in God rather than who we have made ourselves to be.

May we be characterized not by our self-esteem, but by our God-esteem.

In the name of the Father, and of the Son, and of the Holy Spirit. Amen.

On Higher Ground

Redeemed soul, changed heart
set my feet on the pathway called holy
forty years ago.

Pathway rocky, sometimes
hard to traverse, but the Shepherd
leads the way.

Detours that appear easier
always lead to dead ends—no shortcuts
to higher ground.

Always trying to reconcile
Christian talk with Christ-like walk
for that is what

seeking higher ground
is all about. Pressing on, staying true,
relying on Christ

to carry me through to
the place that's called Holy, until my feet
are firmly on Higher Ground.

Be Strong

(NIV) Psalm 27:13 I remain confident of this: I will see the goodness of the LORD in the land of the living. 14 Wait for the LORD; be strong and take heart and wait for the LORD.

I love the Scriptures encouraging us to "be strong." Some people have great physical strength. Others have a mental strength enabling them to overcome difficulties, while still others have a moral strength, sometimes called integrity, that protects them from falling into questionable situations.

Personally, my strength comes from the experience of seeing God work time after time. It is God Who gives me the strength of my convictions, it is the Bible that provides the structure to know who God is, and it is prayer that connects and powers the engine of my life called faith.

So when I am in a season of waiting, I have no need to be anxious because that is when I know that "I can do all things through Christ who strengthens me," and "greater is He that is in me than he that is in the world." And I know, believe and understand that "tribulation works patience, patience experience, and experience hope."

May we each, today and everyday, take joy in waiting for the Lord. And may we remain strong, knowing that hope is on the horizon.

In the name of the Father, and of the Son, and of the Holy Spirit. Amen

Two hundred feet ahead

Ribbon of road stretches
toward tomorrow, night
looms larger, vision
impaired, but car
lights illumine
the path
before me, and
I can see clearly
two hundred feet ahead.

Ribbon of life stretches
toward the unknown,
precarious, ever
changing, vision
impaired, but
God delivers
me through
the dark shadows,
for He can see clearly
the pitfalls ahead.

If I can depend on car
lights to transport me
over potholes and around
the next bend, how much more
can I depend on my Savior,
whose vision is limitless,
whose love never ends.

God is always with me
of that I am sure,
the need to know
unimportant,
the need to see,
petty now. Faith's
headlights shine the way
before me, and I am
two hundred feet closer now.

The Brokenness of Sin

Ps 51:1 (ESV) Have mercy on me, O God,
according to your steadfast love;
according to your abundant mercy
blot out my transgressions.
2 Wash me thoroughly from my iniquity,
and cleanse me from my sin!
3 For I know my transgressions,
and my sin is ever before me…
10 Create in me a clean heart, O God,
and renew a right spirit within me.
11 Cast me not away from your presence,
and take not your Holy Spirit from me.
12 Restore to me the joy of your salvation,
and uphold me with a willing spirit.
13 Then I will teach transgressors your ways,
and sinners will return to you…
17 The sacrifices of God are a broken spirit;
a broken and contrite heart, O God, you will not despise.

When I was a child, we were taught to avoid toys that were cheaply made. And how many times have you had an appliance break down one day after the warranty expired?

But we sometimes forget that it is a good thing for us to allow ourselves to become broken before God. David, the man after God's own heart, understood the brokenness sin brings. And we must learn it is not God Who breaks us but our sin, and if we are not broken by our sin, then we will remain in sin. When we remain in sin, we are separated from God.

God chose David not because he was without sin, but because David knew where to turn for mercy after his sin overshadowed his life. And when David asked for mercy, he had to come face to face with his sin and made the choice to repent.

David understood that repentance was more than saying "I'm sorry." Repentance means we not only have a change of heart, but we turn away from our sin and toward a holy God. Repentance restores us to a right relationship with God. That's the good news.

David was willing to do whatever it takes to come back into relationship with God, and we must do the same. While it is necessary for us to be broken and yield our will to God, we must not stay in our brokenness. Instead, God wants us to live in the joy of our salvation.

Have we recognized what God requires of us? Do we understand that sin breaks us, but repentance restores us. Sin brings a sadness that can lead to death, but repentance brings us back into life and restores the joy of our salvation.

May we bow before a holy God and receive the restoration that can only come through Him.

In the name of the Father, and of the Son, and of the Holy Spirit. Amen.

Never Give Up

The staircase is curved and ornate.
From where I am standing it goes
up, but for one at the top, it comes
down, down to where I am, down

to where my feet meet that first
riser, and I grab the golden railing
as though it is the last thing I will
ever touch, ever hold, and I step,

step up to see what waits above,
beyond what I can comprehend, past
the mundane, superseding the ordinary,
my legs weary but my spirit strong

I pull my way to the top, where
I believe there is light and life,
I continue on, the steps endless
but the exhilaration real now as

I seek some unknown, unnamed
prize at the top of the stairs.

Choosing God

(NIV) Josh 24:13 So I gave you a land on which you did not toil and cities you did not build; and you live in them and eat from vineyards and olive groves that you did not plant.' 14 "Now fear the LORD and serve him with all faithfulness. Throw away the gods your ancestors worshiped beyond the Euphrates River and in Egypt and serve the LORD. 15 But if serving the LORD seems undesirable to you, then choose for yourselves this day whom you will serve, whether the gods your ancestors served beyond the Euphrates, or the gods of the Amorites, in whose land you are living. But as for me and my household, we will serve the LORD."

I heard of a man taking a cruise across the Atlantic. When the cruise ended, the steward found him in his cabin, terribly malnourished. He had to be carried from his room to a hospital. The doctor asked him when was the last time he ate. He answered, "it was the day the ship sailed." When asked why he hadn't eaten, he replied that he only had enough money for the passage--there was nothing left for food. The doctor said, "But sir, your passage includes all of the food you care to eat. You didn't need to pay any more for it--all you had to do was go to the banquet table."

We have been invited to the banquet table. God has called us to glory and virtue, and we have been given the knowledge by God to achieve the kind of character he wants to build in us. Where do we get that knowledge? Part of it comes from the study of His Word. Some of it comes from sitting under scriptural teaching. Part of this knowledge comes by following hard after God.

"Psalms 42:1 As the hart panteth after the water brooks, so panteth my soul after thee, O God. {2} My soul thirsteth for God, for the living God: when shall I come and appear before God?

When we seek hard after God with all of our heart, soul, mind and strength, we will find Him and in finding Him we will see new character traits developing within our own lives. Where there was stress, we will find peace of mind, where there was discontent, we will find delight, where there was doubt, we will find a certainty that surprises even us.

May we let nothing dissuade us from eating at the table set by God.

In the name of the Father, and of the Son, and of the Holy Spirit. Amen.

Perspective

The beauty of a
song that plumbs
the depths
of one's feelings—
nothing like it.

The watercolor of a
landscape that evokes
memories of
your youth—
priceless.

The gift of seeing
the poetry of
words in
everyday situations —
so thankful.

Be Kind

Why are we so critical of others, when
there is so much unfinished work
in our own lives?

How can we see the splinter in another's
eye when the log in our eye obscures
our own vision?

Wouldn't it be remarkable if kindness
instead of criticism
seeped from every pore

and settled on the doorstep
of each person we visited?
Can we just be kind?

Poetry in Memoriam

I am including in "Hope for Tomorrow, Peace for Today" poems I have written through the years to honor friends, family, and acquaintances. It has been my purpose to share with you the means to draw closer to God. I write not because I have all of the answers. Instead, I, like you, am a student, seeking holiness today and every day.

You're Going to Miss Me When I'm Gone
For Mama

Why are mothers so often right? We
laughed together, we cried together, but
more often than not we fought together, not
together against others, but we fought
together with each other, one wanting

to cover her children in bubble wrap to
keep them safe, the other,
wanting to be anything other
than safe. The one thing
we never did was talk together.

We couldn't, not really,
because of her deafness, so we
lived together but apart. Her words,
though, to this day, linger in my heart.
"You're going to miss me when I'm gone."

I wish she had been wrong.

His Little Corner of the World
For Daddy

Sitting on the front porch swing, watching
as his corner of the world grew smaller, and
his kids, at least two of them, grew taller.
He was a simple man, with simple dreams,
and it was enough to listen to the radio for
his baseball teams.

The Travelers and Cardinals, win or lose
it did not matter, it sufficed that they played,
that they would always have another pitcher
and another batter.

He greeted friends and family with a wave
of his hand and an ever so slight self-conscious
grin, for many had surpassed him on this road
of life, but none was any better at dealing
with the strife that sometimes happens,
no matter how hard we try, to live our lives
worthy, to do more than just get by.

I hope he knew his life mattered, because
it mattered to them, the people who knew him
and loved him, the people lucky enough
to call him father and friend.

Gathering Eggs

There was a cow and her calf
which we fed with a bottle, my
sister, my brother, my cousins and I.
And an old plow horse named Daisy
relegated to giving us rides.

There were chickens to feed,
feed to scatter, eggs to gather,
then serve on a platter.
The buildings out back
were just mud and logs,

Places to store potatoes and ham
that came from the hogs.

A root cellar had shelves
For jams and stewed tomatoes
And served as shelter
From the occasional tornado.

We played baseball, had cookouts
Caught lightning bugs in a jar.
Waded barefoot in the creek.
Our entertainment wasn't far.

Thimble, who has the thimble,
A game Gram taught us to play,
But the memory has now
All but faded away.

Lake Nixon
for Aunt Meno

We were taking swimming lessons, my
sister, my cousins and me, and
each time we rounded the bend
in the road, our aunt would
blow the horn.

That third morning I asked why,
why she kept blowing the horn.
"The sign says 'Blow'." We roared
with laughter, could
barely speak.

"No, the sign says 'Slow'."
She was embarrassed, we
were only a little worried knowing
that the person behind the wheel
could not see.

The Blue Room
For Uncle Red

Van Gogh had his blue period
Gainsborough painted "Blue Boy"
But we had our Blue Room
A room brushed blue
By Uncle Red, a man
Of few words and quiet
Demeanor he loved us
And spoiled us and
Colored a room blue
For us.
A man born on Christmas Day
He was a gift to us until the day
He was no more.

I'll Fly Away
For Aunt Mamie, gone too soon

Little twin girls, sitting
in their little twin rockers,
wearing little twin nightgowns,
eyes leaden with sleep.

Daddy, leaning over,
crouching down, crying,
saying, "Aunt Mamie
can't come see you today,
she had to fly away."

"No, she didn't, Daddy,"
my voice strong and
sure. "She promised
she would come."

Mama, in the corner, crying,
peeking out through
her grief-filled handkerchief.

Aunt Mamie would not
be here today, not today
or any more days, she flew
away, oh, glory, she
flew away.

My, how she loved to dance
for Priscilla Dean Mann Miller

She was born more than eight decades ago,
Priscilla Dean, the youngest of ten,
on a rural road in Ellis Township,
now known as Colonel Glenn.

With an inviting smile and golden hair
it is easy to understand why
Theodore Miller, affectionately known as "Ted"
soon found he could not deny

that Priscilla Dean was the girls of his dreams
the one he could not live without.
So they married and started a family
and Dean was completely devout,

for Deborah and Pamela became her life
she was always so proud of them.
She loved her family with all of her heart
and that love never dimmed.

And now her work on earth is done
and her reward is at hand,
She'll be on the front row listening
to Perry Como and Tommy Dorsey's band.

Though she outlived her beloved husband
for more than forty years,
she is now dancing in his arms again
a reunion sweetened with tears.

And all of her precious family
are gathered round to welcome her home
and at the front of the line is Jesus
saying "My child, come kneel before the throne

and I will show you heaven's wonders
so brilliant to behold,
and I promise to take care of your earthly family
until they, too, walk the streets of gold."

Going to sleep and waking up in Heaven
for Ruth Blemmel

Visited a friend yesterday,
a quiet woman, a gentle woman
a woman who has made a difference
in this world.

Body betrayed by the disease within,
she knows her journey here
is almost complete, a new destination
soon at hand.

"I always hoped I would go to sleep
and wake up in heaven," she said,
almost to herself.

Her family by her side, she is comforted
by their presence, they are uplifted
by her spirit letting her calmness
seep into their souls.

And when she takes her final breath,
she will go to sleep and wake up in
Heaven, hand in hand with the One
who died that she might live.

Don't Cry for Me
for Darrell Dover

When the slender thread that ties me
to this earth is severed,
my soul finally will be free
and when I am untethered

I will reach heights that until now
had been beyond my grasp
and surrounded by the light of God
I know that I will clasp

the hand of Jesus as my loved ones
wait to greet me. I will walk among
those gone before
as all of heaven turns out to meet me.

I know you will miss my presence,
and I will miss you, too.
Do not be sad and forlorn,
my love, I will be reunited with you.

But until God is ready to call for you
and your face again I see,
know that I am finally home,
my dear, don't cry for me.

A Glimpse into Heaven
For Charles Cromley

Faith is the substance of things hoped for,
the evidence of things not seen. Heb 11:1

When we at last reach the end
of this temporal existence,
and the beginning of a new
reality somewhere in the distance,
the lines between the two
are sometimes blurred.

He had lain there for days,
unable to say good-bye,
unaware of family, friends,
until abruptly he had eyes
that could see and ears
that could hear

and with a voice strong and clear
sang out, "oh what a foretaste
of glory divine." At a time
when life flowed from him
in dribs and drabs, he was given
a gift, a blessed assurance

of that life to come. And his family,
faithful and loving, shared
in that gift, receiving the tangible
evidence of things not yet seen
through the eyes and ears of one
given a glimpse of heaven.

Where Sickness and Death are no More
For Jackie Dyer

There comes a time in each of our lives
when the silver cord is broken.
Our spirits are at last set free
and though many words are left unspoken,

"I love you," was not one of them, for we
never neglected to say
how much our Nana meant to us
and we will miss her every day.

We know she is in that heavenly land
where sickness and death are no more.
Walking hand in hand with Jesus
she has arrived on that heavenly shore.

The love of her life laughs joyously
as he takes her in his arms
and Nana is suddenly young again,
immune to this world's harms.

We thank God for the time we had together
and though we wish it could have been more,
we know we will be reunited one day
when we walk through heaven's golden door.

Val
For my friend, Val Carr

A woman of uncommon valor, one
whose smile lit up the space,
whose joy was undeniable,
and who possessed both mercy and grace.

She reached out to those who had nothing,
To people others might shun,
Social justice was her passion
and now that her race has been run

there will be a line of people waiting to meet her,
to thank her for doing more than her part,
for being a peacemaker who lived the words of Jesus
and for having the purest of hearts.

For Patti

Unaware of her impact on others,
surprised to see how many care,
she had a welcoming way about her
despite the pain that was always there.

Her smile, so inviting and genuine,
drew us in with its warmth right at the start.
Her hugs which were generous and frequent
Let us know we had a place in her heart.

We were so unprepared to lose her,
but we'll think of her every day.
And we're thankful for the promises of Jesus
to wipe every tear away.

Blanchard and Lynn Causey were the first family I met as an Associate Pastor at Lakewood UMC. A few years after Blanchard succumbed to cancer, his daughter Alyssa followed him into eternity.

Sundown

Sun goes down on the life of a man,
cold dark day yet sunset was grand.
Burdens now lifted; illness departed
still leaving his family brokenhearted.

Another saint goes home, praise God,
Another saint goes home.

Time stands still for those left behind,
clinging to memories, hoping to find
some measure of peace,
some comfort in release.

Another saint goes home, praise God,
another saint goes home.

A life lived with gusto, no need for regret,
redemption assured, Jesus paid the debt.
The struggle now over, the race finally run,
No tears in heaven, a new life begun.

Another saint goes home, praise God,
another saint goes home.

Matt 5:14 You are the light of the world. A city on a hill cannot be hidden. 15Neither do people light a lamp and put it under a basket. Instead, they set it on a lampstand, and it gives light to everyone in the house. 16In the same way, let your light shine before men, that they may see your good deeds and glorify your Father in heaven.

Alyssa's Light

A light that shines even in death
is a gift from the heart of God,
and anyone touched by a ray of that light
has walked where angels trod.

The light of God is eternal
it can never be destroyed
even when the light bearer is with us no more
the radiance still fills us with joy.

We each will grieve her absence
but her incandescence will never dim.
God never reclaims gifts once they are given
for each gift glorifies Him.

So shine on, into the sunset.
Shine on, into the night,
shine on, sweet girl, for we will never forget
the warmth of your God given light.

The Cowboy Code
In memory of Jim Friesz, a Great American Cowboy

Little boys play many games
on the way to becoming men.
But one game will always reign supreme,
the game called Cowboys and Indians.

Many a boy rode a horse made of sticks
and carried a gun filled with caps,
riding the Range in his own backyard
with Roy, Gene and Tom Mix.

The Code of the West was written on their hearts
and was a measure of who they would become
for a Cowboy's ethics were straight and true,
teaching loyalty, courage, and pride in a job well done.

"A man's gotta do what a man's gotta do"
were words many cowboys lived by,
and we continue to celebrate that cowboy spirit,
a spirit that will never die.

On May 3, 2021, I officiated the memorial service of my dear friend, JeanBeth Hill. Less than a year later, I officiated the service of her mother, Betty. In the United Methodist Church, we refer to these services as "A Celebration of Life" and so they are.

Yet, we mourn. Why? Because we love, and we recognize the gulf between life and death will separate us, at least for a time.

The Tie that Binds
For our beloved JeanBeth

She was not granted the gift of years
So here we are, our eyes spilling over with tears.
She held her dear husband and mother close by
But still made room for friends like you and I.

The battles she fought could not be fully shared
The strength she possessed was beyond compare.
Her smile, her laugh and her quick wit, too
Brought us together, yes she was the glue

That made our band of friends work so well
The adventures we had, the stories we still tell
Will live on forever in our hearts and in our minds,
For the love of a friend is truly the tie that binds.

A Quiet Strength
For Betty Hill

There is the strength of the stem to hold up the flower
Even in the midst of the storm
The resolute robin who builds her nest
So that her clutch is safe from harm.

Betty had that same kind of strength
That is forged from the tests of time
The courage of a thousand warriors
But a spirit that was oh so kind,

With a laugh that was infectious
And a twinkle in her eye
She was a daughter, cousin, mother, friend
a faithful Christ follower to the very end.

And when everything was said and done
Christ said, it is time, my child come.

Final Words

Joy Unspeakable

Mortal vessels created for just one purpose,
To house the spirit of the Living God,
Filled with a cleansing fire, renewing fire
Ignited by the Holy Spirit.

Lenten season begins anew, ashes imposed
Upon foreheads as a reminder of our sin
And our mortality, the sign of the cross
The assurance that all is not lost

But indeed, redemption is found.
And during these forty days we
Depart the dryness of sin and sorrow
And seek the Living Water found only

In Christ Jesus. Old things are passed
Away and all things become new
As we reflect on God's goodness
Learning to love the unloveable,

Willing at last to touch the untouchable.
Joy unspeakable and full of glory
As we offer our sacrifice of love
And He raises us from ashes to life.

Praise be to God!

Faith Added to Works

James 2:14-26 (NRSV) 14 What good is it, my brothers and sisters, if you say you have faith but do not have works? Can faith save you? 15 If a brother or sister is naked and lacks daily food, 16 and one of you says to them, "Go in peace; keep warm and eat your fill," and yet you do not supply their bodily needs, what is the good of that? 17 So faith by itself, if it has no works, is dead. 18 But someone will say, "You have faith and I have works." Show me your faith apart from your works, and I by my works will show you my faith. 19 You believe that God is one; you do well. Even the demons believe—and shudder. 20 Do you want to be shown, you senseless person, that faith apart from works is barren? 21 Was not our ancestor Abraham justified by works when he offered his son Isaac on the altar? 22 You see that faith was active along with his works, and faith was brought to completion by the works. 23 Thus the scripture was fulfilled that says, "Abraham believed God, and it was reckoned to him as righteousness," and he was called the friend of God. 24 You see that a person is justified by works and not by faith alone. 25 Likewise, was not Rahab the prostitute also justified by works when she welcomed the messengers and sent them out by another road? 26 For just as the body without the spirit is dead, so faith without works is also dead.

When I first began volunteering at Shelters and Soup Kitchens, I knew intuitively that before I could share the Bread of Life with a lost soul, I first needed to feed that person's body. It felt somehow disingenuous to assure someone that God would supply all of his/her needs according to God's riches in glory, but yet walk away, leaving the person to wonder, "What's wrong with me? I'm hungry, I'm cold, I'm without love. Why won't God supply MY needs?"

And then I look at the letter from James, and I see that bread, and fish, and wine do not just materialize on a table. Instead, God uses Christ followers to put our faith into action and make sure people around us do not do without. God will supply our needs, but many times it is through people like you and me.

I remember reading of John Wesley, the founder of Methodism, and was somewhat startled to learn that Wesley did not begin his ministries because of his faith. Instead, when talking with his brother Charles one day he said, "How will I know when I have done enough?" Charles said, "Enough for what?" John answered, "enough to know I have gained salvation."

You see, John Wesley had opened schools, pharmacies, helped people earn a living so that they could leave the Poor Houses of England, yet his motivation was to gain salvation through his works. It was only after his Aldersgate experience on May 21, 1738, that he said, "I felt I did trust in Christ, Christ alone, for salvation; and an assurance was given me that He had taken away my sins, even mine, and saved me from the law of sin and death." From that moment on, John Wesley ministered in the same manner he had all along, but instead of serving and preaching to gain his own salvation, he did these things because of his salvation.

The battle over James' statement, "Faith by itself, if it has no works, is dead," did not end when James was thrown from the

Temple Mount and then stoned to death because the fall did not kill him. No, the battle still rages today. It is not unusual for those who choose to put their Christian faith to work to be accused of trying to work their way to heaven.

James reminded his readers of the great people of faith found in Hebrews 11. These men and women had not yet seen Jesus, yet because of their faith that the Messiah would come, and their works that were performed as a result of that faith, they were justified by God and welcomed into His Kingdom.

Do you sometimes struggle with your faith? Do you realize that you are not alone? Can I tell you that when you put your faith to work, then your faith will grow larger and larger. Does the work you do replace the faith you have been given? Never. Instead, our work reflects the God who works within us to fulfill His good purpose.

May we put our hands and feet to work, not to gain any glory for ourselves, but so that God shines through us.

In the name of the Father, and of the Son, and of the Holy Spirit. Amen.

Driving Directions

Is there anything more frustrating
than hearing the direction to,
"Turn where the red barn used to be?"

I have heard it said that men
follow directions, women follow landmarks
yet each time I hear that inane phrase

it is uttered from the mouth of a male,
with all seriousness, with no whimsy
intended. How can it be

that a man whose brain works
with logic rather than emotions
(or so I am told)

can possibly believe he is helping
the forlorn traveler with advice
so unaccommodating?

I think the next time someone gives
me directions such as this,
I will turn where the red barn used to be

just to see where it takes me.

Jehovah Nissi, our Banner

Joshua 8 (NIV) 6 Be strong and courageous. Do not be afraid or terrified because of them, for the LORD your God goes with you; he will never leave you nor forsake you."
7 Then Moses summoned Joshua and said to him in the presence of all Israel, "Be strong and courageous, for you must go with this people into the land that the LORD swore to their ancestors to give them, and you must divide it among them as their inheritance. 8 The LORD himself goes before you and will be with you; he will never leave you nor forsake you. Do not be afraid; do not be discouraged."

Have you heard the phrase "swan song?" It is a final gesture one makes before the end—the final soliloquy in a play, the last action one takes, perhaps a good deed. It actually originates from the ancient belief that swans, whose songs are not known to be particularly melodic and sometimes silent altogether, sing a beautiful song while dying.

When I read this chapter in the Old Testament, I feel as though this is Moses' swan song. He is telling the people that his part of this journey is over.

I love the way Moses steps out of the way and ushers Joshua in. From a human perspective I think of all Moses sacrificed to free the Israelites, to lead them through the wilderness for forty years—a disobedient, stubborn people who complained incessantly and returned to their idols whenever Moses was not in their presence.

And then I realize I probably identify more with the Israelites than with Moses. I hope if I had been in his place, and God allowed me only a glimpse of the Promised Land, I could have departed with the same spirit as Moses, but I fear God would have heard a lot of complaining. "But, YHWH, don't you remember all that I did, what about that time...?" Or, God forbid, "I deserve to go."

But, Moses, knowing the battles that faced God's chosen, tells them and Joshua to be strong, reminding them that God would go before them. Jehovah Nissi, God their banner, would go ahead of them, and as long as they proceeded under the banner of God, victory would be theirs.

Even Christ followers can step away from God's banner. We marry the wrong spouse and suffer a lifetime because we believed surely God brought us together; we take the wrong job, and perhaps a series of jobs, but years later realize God was not in those decisions either.

May we, at whatever stage we are in, recognize it is never too late to come under God's banner. Will there still be consequences from not waiting on God? Yes—bad choices produce bad results. But take courage, child of God, the battle is not over, and the victory will be yours.

In the name of the Father, and of the Son, and of the Holy Spirit. Amen.

The Final Goodbye

Writing daily devotionals is easy, but choosing the specific pieces for a book is not so easy. I depend on the One who gives me inspiration for both poetry and devotionals to guide me. I have been blessed to know many wonderful people. May you, and all who read this book, be lifted by His love and covered by His grace.

I pray this book gives you encouragement, and remember: Take the name of Jesus with you and share Him with all you meet.

And may we each know that because of Jesus, we can have Hope for Tomorrow, Peace for Today.

Pastor Carol J. Grace is the author of two books of poetry, "Reflections of a Life Well Spent" and "More Than a Memory." She studied Theology at Hendrix College in Conway, AR and Millsaps College in Jackson, MS., and although retired from preaching full time, still answers calls to visit former parishioners who are hospitalized and is honored to officiate Celebration of Life services.

Carol lives in Little Rock with her husband, Larry, and their four-legged family. Carol and Larry are active members of the Church at Rock Creek.